FIGHTING
TERROR
IN CYBERSPACE

SERIES IN MACHINE PERCEPTION AND ARTIFICIAL INTELLIGENCE*

Editors: **H. Bunke** (Univ. Bern, Switzerland)
P. S. P. Wang (Northeastern Univ., USA)

Vol. 65: Fighting Terror in Cyberspace
(*Eds. M. Last and A. Kandel*)

Vol. 66: Formal Models, Languages and Applications
(*Eds. K. G. Subramanian, K. Rangarajan and M. Mukund*)

Vol. 67: Image Pattern Recognition: Synthesis and Analysis in Biometrics
(*Eds. S. N. Yanushkevich, P. S. P. Wang, M. L. Gavrilova and S. N. Srihari*)

Vol. 68: Bridging the Gap Between Graph Edit Distance and Kernel Machines
(*M. Neuhaus and H. Bunke*)

Vol. 69: Data Mining with Decision Trees: Theory and Applications
(*L. Rokach and O. Maimon*)

Vol. 70: Personalization Techniques and Recommender Systems
(*Eds. G. Uchyigit and M. Ma*)

Vol. 71: Recognition of Whiteboard Notes: Online, Offline and Combination
(*Eds. H. Bunke and M. Liwicki*)

Vol. 72: Kernels for Structured Data
(*T Gärtner*)

Vol. 73: Progress in Computer Vision and Image Analysis
(*Eds. H. Bunke, J. J. Villanueva, G. Sánchez and X. Otazu*)

Vol. 74: Wavelet Theory Approach to Pattern Recognition (2nd Edition)
(*Y. Y. Tang*)

Vol. 75: Pattern Classification Using Ensemble Methods
(*L. Rokach*)

Vol. 76: Automated Database Applications Testing: Specification Representation
for Automated Reasoning
(*R. F. Mikhail, D. Berndt and A. Kandel*)

Vol. 77: Graph Classification and Clustering Based on Vector Space Embedding
(*K. Riesen and H. Bunke*)

Vol. 78: Integration of Swarm Intelligence and Artificial Neural Network
(*Eds. S. Dehuri, S. Ghosh and S.-B. Cho*)

Vol. 79: Document Analysis and Recognition with Wavelet and Fractal Theories
(*Y. Y. Tang*)

Vol. 80: Multimodal Interactive Handwritten Text Transcription
(*V. Romero, A. H. Toselli and E. Vidal*)

Vol. 81: Data Mining with Decision Trees: Theory and Applications
Second Edition
(*L. Rokach and O. Maimon*)

*The complete list of the published volumes in the series can be found at
http://www.worldscientific.com/series/smpai

Series in Machine Perception and Artificial Intelligence – Vol. 65

FIGHTING
TERROR
IN CYBERSPACE

Mark Last & Abraham Kandel

University of South Florida, Tampa, USA

World Scientific

NEW JERSEY · LONDON · SINGAPORE · BEIJING · SHANGHAI · HONG KONG · TAIPEI · CHENNAI

Published by

World Scientific Publishing Co. Pte. Ltd.

5 Toh Tuck Link, Singapore 596224

USA office: 27 Warren Street, Suite 401-402, Hackensack, NJ 07601

UK office: 57 Shelton Street, Covent Garden, London WC2H 9HE

British Library Cataloguing-in-Publication Data
A catalogue record for this book is available from the British Library.

FIGHTING TERROR IN CYBERSPACE
Series in Machine Perception and Artificial Intelligence — Vol. 65

Copyright © 2005 by World Scientific Publishing Co. Pte. Ltd.

ISBN-13 978-981-256-493-1
ISBN-10 981-256-493-4

Printed in Singapore

Preface

The Internet, or the ARPANET in its original name, was a remarkable idea. The Net was designed in the late 60's by US ARPA (Advanced Research Projects Agency) to connect distant computers to each other. This was a critical need at a time when each computer was a precious resource of computing power, which, if connected, could be shared among several groups of researchers at multiple physical sites. Like in many other engineering projects, the ARPANET designers could hardly foresee all future uses of their new infrastructure. Probably, the vision of Internet cafes and airport passengers checking email on their laptops was far beyond their imagination. The fact is that long before computers became affordable and "personal", a major part of the cyberspace traffic shifted from connecting computers engaged in some computationally intensive tasks to connecting the users of those computers — the people. Thus, a special ARPA survey has found in 1973 that as much as three-quarters of all net traffic was nothing more sophisticated than electronic email[1]. Disregarding what ARPA personnel could think or do about it, the cyberspace was moving on its own, hardly controllable way.

Today, in the middle of the first decade of the 21st century, the Internet connects millions of computers worldwide and its traffic originates from unaccounted number of computing applications. The cyberspace has become a major communication medium, where virtually any kind of content can be transferred instantly and reliably between individual users and entire corporations that may be located in totally different corners of the planet. The invention of the World Wide Web (WWW) in the early nineties had a particularly significant effect on the cyberspace evolution. On WWW, the

---

[1] J. Naughton, *A Brief History of the Future: the Origins of the Internet*, Phoenix, 2000, p. 141

person posting the information to a web site, the web site itself (i.e. the web server hosting it), and the visitors of that site do not have to be at any geographical proximity to each other or conform to the same law system. The Net users even do not have to disclose their real identity, not talking about many ways to "spoof" web site names, email addresses, etc.

The continuous and global war on terror, further intensified after the tragic events of September 11, 2001 in the US and more recent acts of violence in Indonesia, Spain, and other countries, does not seem to be directly relevant to the cyberspace revolution. After all, as believed by many, the most dangerous terrorists are hiding in caves or refugee camps with very limited communication capabilities, most of them never use a computer in their life, and even if they do, computer is not a weapon – one cannot kill a massive number of people with a click of a computer mouse! To examine what terrorists really do or don't do on the web, the editors of this volume have organized in April 2004, at Tel-Aviv University, Israel a one-day workshop entitled "Fighting Terror in Cyberspace". The workshop, briefly advertised in the local media, attracted a surprisingly large number of about 200 researchers and professionals, who probably considered the "terror in cyberspace" as something more than just a random combination of unrelated, though popular, terms. The highlights of the talks by workshop speakers, most of whom also contributed the chapters to this volume, were novel and disturbing.

The truth is that the Cyberspace is an ideal environment for international terrorist groups[2] willing to communicate with each other at maximum security and minimal cost. Abe Wagner (Chapter 1) has identified the following four areas of terrorist use (and abuse) of the Internet: covert communications, intelligence gathering on potential targets, propaganda dissemination, and attacks on the Internet itself and the critical infrastructures connected to it. All these activities can be safely conducted under the anonymity cover provided to the web users by Internet cafes, wireless access points, and alias email accounts. Public availability of advanced encryption techniques, including steganography, adds one more powerful level of security to those who have something to hide from the law enforcement authorities. The cyberspace is also a rich source of detailed information on chemical, biological, and even nuclear warfare.

The role of the cyberspace in the global jihad waged by the radical Is-

---

[2]The terrorist organizations mentioned by the authors of this book are included in the list of U.S.-Designated Foreign Terrorist Organizations, which is updated periodically by the U.S. Department of State, Office of Counterterrorism.

lamic terror organizations is analyzed by Shaul Shay in Chapter 2. While disseminating a deep hatred to all attributes of the Western culture, the Al-Qaeda organization has already proven its efficiency in exploiting the Western technology for its own needs. The Internet, as an infrastructure designed by the US Department of Defense, is not an exception: Al-Qaeda operatives are widely using it for exchanging encoded messages that contain seemingly innocent content and gaining background information prior to terrorist attacks. The brutal footages of hostage killings by Iraqi insurgents have recently demonstrated the crucial role of the cyberspace as a battlefield in psychological warfare, which is a core activity of any terrorist organization.

It is time to ask ourselves a legitimate question: are we going to lose this information battle in the medium created by the best of our own minds? Are we going to lose the cyberspace to the stateless, yet smart and ruthless, enemy? The information battles of the 21st century can be fought and won by no other means but information technology. Chapter 3 by Mark Last explains the potential contribution of the state-of-the-art data mining techniques to the central tasks of cyber security and cyber intelligence. With data mining tools, the counter-terrorist agencies can discover hidden links between seemingly unrelated individuals, effectively monitor dynamic content of terrorist web sites, identify changes and trends in web documents posted by terrorist organizations, and detect dangerous anomalies in the behavior of mission-critical software systems that may be subject to cyber attacks.

Chapter 4 by Bracha Shapira presents a content-based model for monitoring web users that may be involved in terrorist activities while visiting numerous web sites maintained by various terrorist organizations. The model feasibility stems from the well-known fact that users' surfing interests tend to conform to relatively stable patterns. Different groups of users usually differ in the content of web sites they normally visit. The normal profile of a group can be induced by the data mining methodology of cluster analysis and then used to detect any suspicious deviation from the norm.

Chapter 5 by Yuval Elovici shows how the model of Chapter 4 is implemented as the core methodology of the Terrorist Detection System (TDS), which is aimed at tracking down suspects that access terrorist-related content on the web. The initial experiments with the system, based on the web content log of a group of university students, have shown significant improvement vs. a state-of-the-art anomaly detection system, which used only Operating System commands issued by the users.

A further improvement in anomaly detection performance when analyzing web content is reached in Chapter 6 (by Menahem Friedman, Moti Schneider, and Abraham Kandel) via novel clustering techniques based on fuzzy logic. This is not a surprising result, since fuzzy logic and fuzzy set theory are known to be particularly efficient for modeling approximate concepts such as similarity of web documents.

In Chapter 7 of this volume, Yehuda Shaffer describes one of the most important aspects in the global war on terror – detecting and stopping the terror financing. All known techniques of money laundering developed by criminal networks are implemented, and sometimes enhanced by terrorist organizations. This is a truly information combat, since most suspicious funds are transferred electronically. As indicated by Shaffer, a growing part of financial information is transferred via the Internet.

Though English is still the leading language of the Internet, web documents in foreign languages are important sources of information on international terrorist groups. Along with developing new automated translation tools, the research community is currently focused on direct detection, extraction, and summarization of documents in multiple languages. In Chapter 8, Alex Markov and Mark Last describe a novel, graph-based methodology for cross-lingual classification of web documents. The methodology has reached high accuracy rates on a collection of authentic web documents in Arabic.

The goal of this book is to present an up-to-date survey of threats, challenges, and tools in cyber warfare on terror. As information technology continues to move forward and become more affordable for people around the world, the threats of cyber terror in all its forms can be expected to grow, along with our capability to develop more sophisticated tools than can detect, analyze, and prevent these malicious activities. We have to face the reality: there *are* terrorists in cyber space, or "cyber caves" if you wish.

Acknowledgments

We thank all the contributing authors who, despite their busy schedule, have responded enthusiastically to our invitation by giving a presentation at the Fighting Terror in Cyberspace Workshop and then submitting a chapter to this volume. We would also like to thank Marina Litvak who has done the final formatting of the book. The preparation of this volume was partially supported by the Fulbright Foundation that has granted Prof.

Kandel the Fulbright Research Award at Tel-Aviv University, Faculty of Engineering during the academic year 2003-2004.

Mark Last and Abraham Kandel June 2005

Contents

Preface   v

1. Terrorism and the Internet: Use and Abuse   1
   Abraham R. Wagner

   1.1 Introduction   1
       1.1.1 Evolution of Cyberspace and the Internet   1
       1.1.2 A Paradigm Shift and Exponential Grown
             in Cyberspace   5
   1.2 Terrorist Use of the Internet   7
       1.2.1 Terrorist Use of the Internet for Covert Communications 8
       1.2.2 Finding Terrorist E-Mail 12
       1.2.3 The Impact of Encryption 13
       1.2.4 Non E-mail Techniques 16
   1.3 Terrorist Access to Information 17
       1.3.1 Potential Targets for Future Attacks 17
       1.3.2 Logistics for Terrorist Operations 18
       1.3.3 Technical Data for Terrorist Operations 19
   1.4 Terrorist Web Sites 20
       1.4.1 Platform for Terrorist Propaganda 21
       1.4.2 Platform for Terrorist Recruitment and Fundraising . 22
   1.5 Terrorists and Cyber-Terrorism 24

Bibliography   27

2. The Radical Islam and the Cyber Jihad   29

Shaul Shay

2.1 The New Trends of Terror   29
2.2 Information Terrorism   31
2.3 The Cyberspace as Battlefield   33
    2.3.1 Netwars and Networks   33
    2.3.2 The Cyberspace as Cyber-Jihad   33
    2.3.3 The Trends in the Information Age   34
2.4 Conclusion   35

Bibliography   39

3. Using Data Mining Technology for Terrorist Detection on
    the Web   41

    Mark Last

3.1 Introduction: Who is Hiding in Cyber Caves?   41
3.2 Data Mining for Countering Terror in Cyberspace   43
    3.2.1 Taxonomy of Data Mining Methods   43
    3.2.2 Data Mining Needs and Challenges for Cyber Security
           and Cyber Intelligence   46
3.3 Key Techniques of Cyber Warfare   47
    3.3.1 Link Analysis   47
    3.3.2 Information Agents   49
    3.3.3 Trend Discovery   52
    3.3.4 Real-Time Data Mining   53
    3.3.5 Input-Output Analysis of Software Systems   56
3.4 Summary   58

Bibliography   59

4. A Content-Based Model for Web-Monitoring   63

    Bracha Shapira

4.1 Introduction   63
4.2 Detailed Description of the Model   66
    4.2.1 Learning Phase   66
    4.2.2 The Detection Phase   68
4.3 Summary   69

Bibliography 73

5. TDS — An Innovative Terrorist Detection System 75
   Yuval Elovici

   5.1 Introduction 75
   5.2 Content-Based Methodology for Anomaly Detection: Review 76
       5.2.1 Learning the Normal User Behavior 77
       5.2.2 Detecting Abnormal Users 78
   5.3 Design Goals 79
   5.4 TDS Architecture 79
       5.4.1 On-line HTML Tracer 81
       5.4.2 Vectorization 81
       5.4.3 Normal User Behavior Computation 82
       5.4.4 Detection 82
   5.5 Performance Measures 83
   5.6 System Evaluation 84
   5.7 System Deployment 85
   5.8 Summary 87

Bibliography 89

6. Clustering Algorithms for Variable-Length Vectors and
   Their Application to Detecting Terrorist Activities 91
   Menahem Friedman

   Moti Schneider

   Abraham Kandel

   6.1 Introduction 91
   6.2 Creating the Centroids 94
   6.3 Application 99
       6.3.1 Clustering 99
       6.3.2 Detection 100
   6.4 The Experiment 100
   6.5 Summary 101

Bibliography 103

7. Analysis of Financial Intelligence and the Detection of
    Terror Financing   105
    Yehuda Shaffer

    7.1 Introduction 105
    7.2 Implementation of International Anti Money
         Laundering Standards in the Combat Against
         Terror Financing 106
         7.2.1 The Impact of 9/11 106
         7.2.2 Money Laundering and Terror Financing 107
    7.3 Terror Financing Typologies 107
         7.3.1 Characteristics of Terror (Not Only Terrorist)
                Financing 107
         7.3.2 Why and How Do Terror Groups Launder Money . . 108
    7.4 Reporting Duties of Financial Institutions and the Role
         of Financial Intelligence Units (FIU) in Combating
         Terror Financing 110
         7.4.1 A Strategy for Fighting Terror Financing 110
         7.4.2 Information Received from the Private Sector 111
         7.4.3 The Role of the FIU 112
         7.4.4 IT Analysis Tools at FIUs 113
         7.4.5 Terror Financing Investigation 114
    7.5 Information Available - Possible Future Developments . . . 114

8. Identification of Terrorist Web Sites with Cross-Lingual
    Classification Tools   117
    Alex Markov and Mark Last

    8.1 Introduction 117
    8.2 Document Categorization and Classification 119
    8.3 Selected Applications of Web Document Classification . . . 119
         8.3.1 Automatic Web News Extraction 120
         8.3.2 Personalization and E-Commerce 121
         8.3.3 Organization of Web Document Collections 121
         8.3.4 Multi-Lingual Applications 122
    8.4 Document Representation 123
         8.4.1 Traditional Text Models 123
         8.4.2 Web Document Models 124
    8.5 Graph Based Representations of Web Documents 125

8.5.1   Graph Structure   125
8.5.2   Term Extraction Methods   128
        8.5.2.1   Naïve Extraction   128
        8.5.2.2   Smart Extraction   128
8.5.3   Frequent Sub-Graph Extraction Problem   129
8.6   Cross-Lingual Web Document Classification with Graphs   .   130
8.6.1   Representation and Classification Process   130
8.6.2   Web Document Representation Example   132
8.7   Case Study: Identification of Terrorist Web Sites in Arabic   136
8.7.1   About Document Collection   136
8.7.2   Preprocessing of Documents in Arabic   137
8.7.3   Experiment and Evaluation of Results   138
8.8   Conclusions   140
8.9   Acknowledgment   141

Bibliography   143

Appendix A   Useful Sources   147

Appendix B   Terrorist Web Sites — Examples   149

Appendix C   About the Authors   157

Index   165

Chapter 1

Terrorism and the Internet: Use and Abuse

Abraham R. Wagner

System Research & Development Corp. Los Angeles, CA 90067
E-mail: arw@it.org

1.1 Introduction

What began as an MIT doctoral dissertation in 1962, and a U.S. Defense
Department experiment in communications in the years that followed, has
evolved into a technological revolution now known as "cyberspace" and the
Internet. It is indeed a revolution that goes far beyond communications.
In terms of making media available to people worldwide, it is likely the
most significant advance since Gutenberg's invention of moveable type in
the 15th century. Use of the Internet has literally exploded from a handful
of scientists in the U.S. to a world where "net" access is almost universal.
The net has become a medium for all – the good, the bad and the ugly,
and terrorists are no exception. Terrorists, terrorist organizations and their
sponsors have all become increasing users of the Internet for a variety of
functions. Just as in years past, when terrorists relied on other technologies
such as telephone, radio, the mails and other systems, they cannot be barred
from net access and will continue to use net resources for their purposes.
The present paper explores the evolution of the Internet; current terrorist
uses of the net; and what may be possible in terms of counter-terrorist
operations in this area.

1.1.1 *Evolution of Cyberspace and the Internet*

True revolutions in communications do not come along very often. Possibly the only thing that comes close in comparison to the Internet was

1

Morse's invention of the telegraph in the early 19th Century [1]. At the out-set, e-mail and the web were not even a part of the vision. Cyberspace and the Internet began as another "project" between the U.S. Defense Depart-ment's Advanced Research Projects Agency (ARPA) and a research group around the Massachusetts Institute of Technology [2]. Leonard Klienrock's now famous MIT thesis presented a novel and remarkable new concept for communications, namely that "packet switching" would be a more efficient use of a network than "line switching" that had been the approach taken since the time of Morse [3]. Klienrock's 1962 thesis did not lead immediately to the ARPANET or the Internet. Communications in general were not a high priority for ARPA in the 1960s, and the space race got most of the Agency's attention and funding. In those years the U.S. was sadly behind the Soviet Union, and was rushing madly to catch up. In late 1966 ARPA did propose a new communications program to the U.S. Congress, and sought additional funds for the next fiscal year to begin work on an experi-mental switched packet network. Given the pace of the U.S. Governmental process in those years, funds for the ARPA Communications Program were not actually available until 1968, at which the Agency solicited proposals from various contractors to build the first elements of the ARPANET [4]. By

---

[1] In May 1844 Samuel Morse sent his famous message "What hath God wrought" over a 37-mile telegraph line from Washington to Baltimore, funded by a 50, 000 grant from the U.S. Army. Although ignored in the first few years, by 1851 there were 50 competing telegraph companies, and by 1866 Western Union (formed by a merger of several of these) had over 4,000 offices and had become the first communications giant in history.

[2] Formed during the Cold War, in an effort to fund a wide range of defense technolo-gies of possible importance to the U.S., ARPA has been at the forefront of technical developments in a host of critical areas. Over the years, the word "Defense" has been added, then subtracted, and then added again to its name, and it is currently known as DARPA. In the early days of the net, the "D" wasn't there, so the net was known as the ARPANET. DARPA itself does no work internally. Its relatively small staff of technical experts is responsible for the direction of research funds to universities, contractors, na-tional laboratories and others who perform the actual research tasks. The results have been nothing less than astounding. This approach has given rise to an entire informa-tion technology industry, and several others. For a good historical account, see Stephen Segaller, Nerds 2.0.1: A Brief History of the Internet, New York: TV Books, 1998.

[3] In simple terms, "line switching" means that the sender and recipient are somehow "connected" for the duration of their communication, and tie up the line for that period. Alternatively, the "packet switching" concept breaks all communications into uniform digital "packets" which are sent over available network resources, and then re-assembled by the recipient. No single line is tied up, and the network routs the packets in the most efficient way possible. In the analog world of the 1960s, it was an interesting concept, but of limited practical use. In the digital world of the 1990s, it became a multi-billion dollar revolution. It has changed both the technology and economics of communications as nothing else in history.

[4] ARPA's request for proposals, issued in July 1968, went to a range of companies. It is interesting to note that the "major" firms IBM and Digital Equipment Corp. both

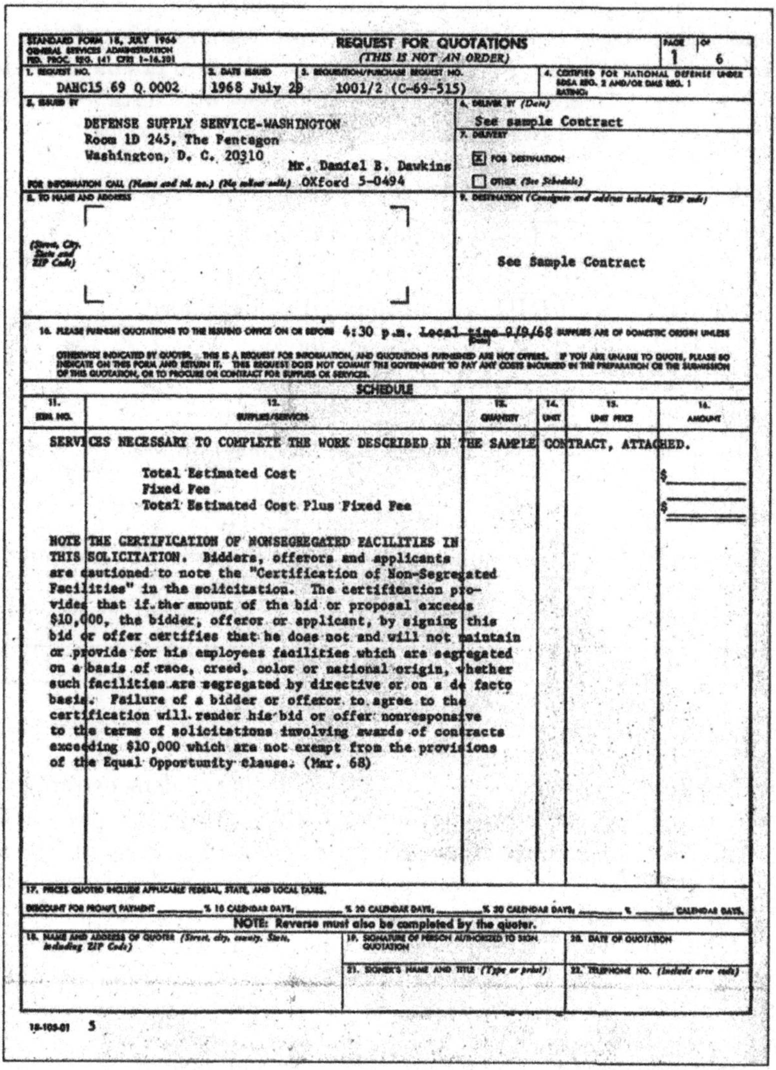

STANDARD FORM 18, JULY 1966
GENERAL SERVICES ADMINISTRATION
FED. PROC. REG. (41 CFR) 1-16.201

REQUEST FOR QUOTATIONS
(THIS IS NOT AN ORDER)

PAGE 1 OF 6

1. REQUEST NO. DAHC15 69 Q 0002
2. DATE ISSUED 1968 July 29
3. REQUISITION/PURCHASE REQUEST NO. 1001/2 (C-69-515)
4. CERTIFIED FOR NATIONAL DEFENSE UNDER BDSA REG. 2 AND/OR DMS REG. 1 RATING:

5. ISSUED BY
DEFENSE SUPPLY SERVICE-WASHINGTON
Room 1D 245, The Pentagon
Washington, D. C. 20310

6. DELIVER BY (Date) See sample Contract

7. DELIVERY
[X] FOR DESTINATION
[ ] OTHER (See Schedule)

FOR INFORMATION CALL (Name and tel. no.) (No collect calls) Mr. Daniel B. Dawkins OXford 5-0494

8. TO NAME AND ADDRESS (Street, City, State and ZIP Code)

9. DESTINATION (Consignee and address including ZIP code)
See Sample Contract

10. PLEASE FURNISH QUOTATIONS TO THE ISSUING OFFICE ON OR BEFORE 4:30 p.m. Local time 9/9/68 (Date) SUPPLIES ARE OF DOMESTIC ORIGIN UNLESS OTHERWISE INDICATED BY QUOTER. THIS IS A REQUEST FOR INFORMATION, AND QUOTATIONS FURNISHED ARE NOT OFFERS. IF YOU ARE UNABLE TO QUOTE, PLEASE SO INDICATE ON THIS FORM AND RETURN IT. THIS REQUEST DOES NOT COMMIT THE GOVERNMENT TO PAY ANY COSTS INCURRED IN THE PREPARATION OR THE SUBMISSION OF THIS QUOTATION, OR TO PROCURE OR CONTRACT FOR SUPPLIES OR SERVICES.

SCHEDULE

11. ITEM NO.	12. SUPPLIES/SERVICES	13. QUANTITY	14. UNIT	15. UNIT PRICE	16. AMOUNT
	SERVICES NECESSARY TO COMPLETE THE WORK DESCRIBED IN THE SAMPLE CONTRACT, ATTACHED.				
	Total Estimated Cost				$____
	Fixed Fee				
	Total Estimated Cost Plus Fixed Fee				$____

NOTE THE CERTIFICATION OF NONSEGREGATED FACILITIES IN THIS SOLICITATION. Bidders, offerors and applicants are cautioned to note the "Certification of Non-Segregated Facilities" in the solicitation. The certification provides that if the amount of the bid or proposal exceeds $10,000, the bidder, offeror or applicant, by signing this bid or offer certifies that he does not and will not maintain or provide for his employees facilities which are segregated on a basis of race, creed, color or national origin, whether such facilities are segregated by directive or on a de facto basis. Failure of a bidder or offeror to agree to the certification will render his bid or offer nonresponsive to the terms of solicitations involving awards of contracts exceeding $10,000 which are not exempt from the provisions of the Equal Opportunity clause. (Mar. 68)

17. PRICES QUOTED INCLUDE APPLICABLE FEDERAL, STATE, AND LOCAL TAXES.
DISCOUNT FOR PROMPT PAYMENT ____ % 10 CALENDAR DAYS; ____ % 20 CALENDAR DAYS; ____ % 30 CALENDAR DAYS; ____ % ____ CALENDAR DAYS.

NOTE: Reverse must also be completed by the quoter.

18. NAME AND ADDRESS OF QUOTER (Street, city, county, State, including ZIP Code)
19. SIGNATURE OF PERSON AUTHORIZED TO SIGN QUOTATION
20. DATE OF QUOTATION
21. SIGNER'S NAME AND TITLE (Type or print)
22. TELEPHONE NO. (Include area code)

18-103-01 5

Fig. 1.1 ARPA Request for Proposals to build the ARPAnet and the BBN proposal to build the first ARPAnet nodes

---

declined to bid, stating their belief that this was an impossible task. The one proposal received, and subsequently funded, came from Bolt Beranek and Newman (BBN), of Cambridge, MA. Not surprisingly, the BBN personnel who wrote the proposal, and went on the build the ARPANET, were a group closely linked to MIT and had developed the switched packet concept for several years preceding. Even so, the BBN team had

September 1968 ARPA had funded a team at Bolt, Baranek and Newman of Cambridge, MA to build the first network processors and install them at UCLA and Stanford (See Figure 1.1). Despite their own doubts that such a system could actually be built, the first processors were installed in 1969, and connected by a 56 KB leased-line between these first nodes [5].

Year	Nodes	Events
1969	4	UCLA, Stanford, UCSB, Utah; net 56kb
1970	5	BBN added; net spans U.S.
1971	15	MIT, Rand, Harvard, others added
1974	62	TCP protocol developed
1977	111	Apple II launched as PC
1981	213	Microsoft has 40 employees
1983	562	TCP/IP protocols developed; Internet is born
1984	1,024	Domain names invented (.com)
1986	5,000	First bulletin board with GUI
1987	10,000	25-million PCs sold in US; net is T1 (1.54mb)
1989	100,000	ARPAnet de-installed; now Internet
1992	1,000,000	Mosaic browser developed
2004	Unknown	Internet is a global resource

Fig. 1.2   Nodes on the Net

Even after the initial prototypes had been built and demonstrated, the net did not expand with any great speed, and received little notice outside the scientific and research community. Electronic mail (e-mail) was not even part of the initial ARPAnet concept, and was in fact developed by one contractor employee on his own. Likewise media files and the "web" were never a part of the original concept as well, and it would be some years before these features that revolutionized communications and the media were developed. As Figure 1.2 illustrates, the early years of the net were characterized by relatively few "nodes" and users, largely institutions that were DARPA contractors. The exponential growth of the net was really the result of some other technology developments, the most important of which was the so-called personal computer, or PC. While most early efforts

---

serious doubts that the system could be built, particularly in the time frame ARPA had specified.

[5]Dr. Kleinrock, then at UCLA, was given the honor of attempting the world's first login. In a well-known story, he typed in "LOGIN" at which point the system crashed. A recovery was successful, and the first nodes of the net were up and running, with two additional nodes (UCSB and Utah) added later in the year.

to build low-cost computers were failures, or at best resulted in machines that were popular only with hobbyists, the real "breakthrough" came in the form of the Apple II launched in 1977. Within a few years this was followed by the IBM PC, and included an operating system (Microsoft DOS) and applications such as a spreadsheet (VisiCalc) and word processing (Word) that made the PC a useful device for both offices and homes. By the late 1980s millions of PCs were being sold in the U.S. What remained to happen was a means to connect this vast and growing number of computers to the net. A few related technology developments, such as the local area net (LAN); the modem; and the emergence of commercial network service providers (such as Prodigy and AOL) gave the broad population a means to access the net, heretofore limited to a few ARPA researchers. With the passage of the Strategic Computing Act in 1988 the ARPAnet transitioned to the Internet, and funding was provided to advance the use of the net in a wide number of areas [6].

1.1.2 *A Paradigm Shift and Exponential Grown in Cyberspace*

As illustrated above the Internet explosion of the last decade, which is truly a paradigm shift in science and technology, is not the result of a single discovery or event. It is more the convergence of a few separate but related developments taking place at about the same time. It is possible to view this "explosion" in terms of four key technology developments.

Moore's Law – Cheap Computers for Everybody: Named after Gordon Moore, a co-inventor of the integrated circuit and a founder of Intel, the world entered an era of increasingly cheap and powerful integrated circuits or processors. Intel's original 8080 series of powerful, low-cost microprocessors and its successors over the years made possible the PC and a myriad of workstations, laptops, PDAs and other devices. The world entered the age of "free hardware."

Packet Switching: The new era of switched packed communications envisioned by Len Klienrock, Vint Cerf, Bob Kahn and others brought about a true communications revolution. The computers and the infrastructure were rapidly moving into place. Now they could all be connected into a worldwide network.

Digital Everything: At the same time computers, storage and communications were evolving, the information age was moving rapidly from an

---

[6]The principal sponsor of this law in the U.S. Senate was Senator Albert Gore, Jr. While Gore later misstated in his unsuccessful Presidential Campaign that he had "invented" the Internet, he was indeed largely responsible for its successful evolution, and the world is indebted to Sen. Gore for this.

analog world into a digital one. Data, voice, video, text, images, movies
– it didn't matter. Whatever "it" was, it was now being done in a digital form. For the research community, the major obstacle for generations
had been the analog-to-digital conversion. Almost overnight the problem
of A/D conversion was vanishing. Analog anything was quickly vanishing.

Infinite/cheap Bandwidth: New developments in communications such
as fiber optic cable, advanced RF systems and satellite transponders
brought about an economic revolution, if not a technical one as well in
worldwide availability of commercial bandwidth. The availability of order-
of-magnitude greater, and high-quality bandwidth worldwide caused yet
another revolution in the economics of telecommunication. The result was
far lower costs, and for Internet users a truly remarkable phenomenon – virtually free worldwide communications. It was now possible to send e-mail,
files, and other digital materials to any Internet address, at no marginal
cost. Users only needed Internet access [7].

The combination of these factors has been a truly exponential growth
in cyberspace. The world has moved from one that was only recently dominated by analog systems, paper files, and other technologies dating to
biblical times to one now dominated by networked computer systems and
digital everything. Communications, information, finance, control, national
security and even our social lives are now involved with net-based systems
to a greater or lesser extent – and greater in more cases daily. Aside from
this being a technological revolution, it has truly become a social, cultural
and economic one as well. Using the vernacular, people have really become
"hooked" on these capabilities for a number of reasons:

- Free, asynchronous communications (e-mail) has become increasingly popular. It doesn't require the sender and receiver to be
  on-line at the same time.
- Net-based communications make things easier, not harder. Sending
  information, documents, photos, etc. immediately, for free, at the
  click of a mouse has great appeal. In the "old days" people had
  to print documents, ship documents and files, spend money, and it
  took time to happen. Better, faster and for free has become very
  popular – and for good reason.
- The explosive movement of much media to web-based systems has
  made possible free and low-cost access to a wide range of information. The entire concept of information science, libraries and

---

[7]The final results of this revolution in the economics of telecommunications have still
not been seen. Most carriers evolved on the basis of being able to charge individual
users for service. International telex, telephone, FAX, etc. were a major revenue base
for these carriers. Since Internet users were now paying nothing to the carriers to send
the same (or much more!) data a significant problem has evolved.

research has changed radically.

1.2 Terrorist Use of the Internet

While the first users of "the net" were researchers affiliated with DARPA and the U.S. DoD, Internet use has spread across the globe. Indeed, net use is not only found in the developed world, but even in the most desolate areas of the Third World, and users include people of all ages and from all walks of life – including terrorists. Indeed, as one analyst has written "Cyberspace is not only a nascent forum for political extremists to propagate their messages but also a medium for strategic and tactical innovation in their campaigns against enemies." [8].

In many ways the Internet and similar networked systems are ideal for terrorist activities and operations. At the most general level, they provide capabilities for worldwide communications and security at exceedingly low cost. This concept is certainly no secret, and recent evidence demonstrates widespread net use by various terrorist organizations worldwide. The analysis below is focused on terrorist use (and abuse) of the Internet in four major areas:

- Use of the Internet for terrorist communications, essentially covert communications, and as a means for a new command and control infrastructure.
- Access to information via the Internet and world wide web (WWW), including for such requirements as information on potential targets as well as technical data in areas such as weapons construction
- Use of the Internet as a platform for the dissemination of propaganda on terrorist groups and causes, and the related objective of recruiting individuals into these organizations
- Terrorist attacks on the Internet, and capabilities connected to the net – commonly known as cyber warfare, as yet another avenue for terrorist attack.

In the Middle East, for example, both secular and Islamist terrorist organizations have increasingly employed net-based systems and practices to achieve their political ends. These capabilities not only provide the terrorists with greater flexibility and security, but also open up a much broader

---

[8]Col. (R.) Sami Barak, "Between Violence and 'e-jihad': Middle Eastern Terror Organizations in the Information Age," in Lars Nicander and Magnus Ransdorp, Terrorism in the Information Age – New Fromtiers? (Stockholm, Swedish National Defence College, 2004).

range of opportunities for targeting and attack, due to a diffusion of command and control [9].

1.2.1 Terrorist Use of the Internet for Covert Communications

It would be truly difficult to envision a more ideal medium for terrorist communications than the modern Internet [10]. As with any other user, today's Internet offers the terrorist asynchronous worldwide service, with global access. The sender and recipient of an e-mail or net-based file transfer can be any place, at any time. How could any self-respecting terrorist ask for more? At the same time, Internet services are close to free and, as previously discussed, available bandwidth is virtually unlimited. For example, the Hamas terrorist organization has for a number of years utilized the Internet to send password-protected files and messages to their members relative to attacks, including maps, photographs, directions, codes and technical details for various operations [11].

To fully appreciate the benefits that the Internet has brought to terrorists in this area it is necessary to consider the obstacles that such groups and individuals face in this area, generally known as "covert communications." As with other covert operatives, such as those in intelligence services or the military, there is a need to communicate reliably and effectively, while avoiding either detection (location) or having ones communications intercepted by hostile forces – which in the case of the terrorists are the intelligence services, military, and law enforcement agencies of target nations. In years past, terrorists and intelligence operatives alike have employed all sorts of methods to communicate, ranging from human (and some non-human) messengers to a wide array of technologies [12]. Virtually all of these

---

[9]See Michael Whine, "Cyberspace: A New Medium for Communication, Command and Control by Extremists," May 5, 1999 at www.ict.org.il.

[10]Digital cell phones and PDAs operating on GSM systems are a useful adjunct to the Internet, but do not offer the same level security and capability at the net. Indeed, the increasing ability of the world's intelligence services to access cell phones has not been lost on the terrorists. They continue to use them, but now do so in ways that minimizes their vulnerability. If nothing else, they change their SIM cards and related numbers with great frequency to avoid detection!

[11]Col. (R.) Sami Barak, "Between Violence and 'e-jihad': Middle Eastern Terror Organizations in the Information Age," in Lars Nicander and Magnus Ransdorp, Terrorism in the Information Age – New Frontiers? (Stockholm, Swedish National Defence College, 2004). See also "Cyber Terrorism," Foreign Report (London), September 25, 1997. Hamas leader Abd-al-Rahman Zaydan was convicted in 1995 on the basis of information stored on his personal computer, which included a database linking Hamas squads and terrorists in Israel, Jordan and Germany. Reported in Yediot Ahronot, January 1, 1996.

[12]Some of these have actually been quite clever, such as using coded messages on the

methods suffered from one or more serious problems:

- They were not reliable, or could not assure the recipient would receive the information, either in a timely manner or at all.
- Almost none were truly secure [13]. Most telecommunications systems, particularly analog ones, have long been subject to geolocation and intercept by foreign intelligence services. Modern terrorists have come to appreciate this capability and have adjusted their operations accordingly [14].
- Highly specialized systems used by the military and intelligence services of advanced nations are not commercially available, and the secure systems that are commercially available are costly and relatively cumbersome.

Compared to the early methods, or even the very costly and sophisticated systems used by advanced nations, the Internet is a dream come true. As with any other user, the net provides asynchronous service with global access. The sender and recipient can be any place, at any time, and do not need to link up at a specific time, as would be the case with a telephone call. The cost of net access is close to nothing. For most terrorist communications, bandwidth is not a major issue, so dial-up access is sufficient, and can be accomplished using phone POPs and servers in distant locations. Laptops and other forms of personal computers are widely available throughout the world at low prices. Dial-in access to any number of Internet providers from almost any phone on earth is not costly either [15]. For those terrorists without a computer or a phone line, the proliferation of Internet cafes enables them to access messages with ease. Beyond the low cost of net access, the Internet is probably more reliable than any other system in existence. It is a design feature of switched packet communications. The net degrades by using alternate paths and moving more slowly, rather than

---

weather forecasts of local radio stations to pass operational signals.

[13] As a practical matter, it has been known for centuries how to generate an unbreakable code for secure communications. This is known as a "one time pad." Unfortunately, the process is administratively cumbersome, to say the least, since the code or pad needs to be changed for every message, and any message needs to be very short, and not exceed the key length on the pad.

[14] Following the attack on the La Belle Disco in Germany by Libyan terrorists, President Reagan authorized the release of communications intelligence information collected by the U.S. against Libya as a part of his justification for retaliatory air strikes against Libya. While it served the political purposes of the time, it also served as a "wake up" call to terrorists that the U.S. was indeed paying considerable attention to their communications, and it was necessary for them to change their mode of operations.

[15] Note for example the number of international dial-in points-of-presence or "POPs" that America on Line (AOL) maintains.

simply failing as in the case of line-switched or point-to-point systems [16].

Access to the Internet itself is accomplished in several ways, including to most common commercial methods and some adjuncts:

High bandwidth, direct connections: From the evidence available, few terrorists themselves have high-bandwidth DSL or similar sorts of direct Internet access that they use for covert communications purposes. It may be the case that specific individuals have some other job that provides them with direct high-speed access, although such cases are probably uncommon. Here it is important to distinguish terrorist operatives conducting covert communications from major terrorist organizations and their affiliates that maintain web sites for propaganda and other purposes, having established sites, servers and direct Internet connections. These are discussed further in Section 1.4 below.

Dial-up services: For the most part, terrorists rely heavily on dial-up services, either using land line or cellular telephone connections. Aside from cost and convenience factors, this method affords an additional layer of security. It is possible to dial a local access number or "POP" from virtually anywhere there is telephone service [17]. The POP is little more than a modem with a phone line, and does not record the phone numbers of incoming calls. As a practical matter, a terrorist can dial a POP in virtually any city, and simply pay the long distance charges, and the net has no way of tracing where any given e-mail actually originated. In remote areas, where there is telephone service but no direct Internet service, this raises some risk, which terrorists appear to be avoiding now by sending disks with their e-mail and data elsewhere for transmission [18].

Internet Cafes: The proliferation of public Internet access, largely in Internet cafes, has proved popular with terrorists in the Middle East, Africa and elsewhere. Clearly an individual can enter an Internet café, check his or her e-mail at whatever account they are currently using, and depart. Aside

---

[16] In the lore of U.S. Defense Department history it has been said that the ARPAnet was built to provide reliable communications in the case of nuclear war. While it may provide this feature, it simply isn't correct. Switched packet communications began as an experiment in the optimization of network resources, which worked, and not as a program in communications survivability. See here Segaller, Nerds 2.0.1: A Brief History of the Internet., op. cit.

[17] The GSM systems in use in large parts of the world actually distinguish between voice and data calls, and in many cases only permit data calls on cell phones where there is an established account, rather than the "pre-paid" accounts, where there is no accounting for who has any given cell phone number. This is, however, not universal, and seems to be going away as carriers are fighting for business.

[18] Clearly this slows down the process, but avoids a major risk. It appears that this is the method currently being used by Osama bin Laden for much of his communications. Reports in the New York Times in July 2004 from a captured operative indicated that two sets of couriers were bringing his disks to Islamabad, Pakistan for transmission there.

from any appeal as a movie script, this method is certainly low-cost and relatively safe. There are some limitations in terms of file sizes, printers etc., but are quite useful for less complex communications.

Unwitting servers: Hacking into an unwitting server and using it as a covert mail host is a possible technique, but from most evidence is more of a hacker's exercise than a method employed by terrorists with regularity. By and large terrorists can be seen as reasonably intelligent Internet users, but not terribly sophisticated in terms of "hacking" and illicit net uses.

Wireless Internet, and other web-enabled devices: Wireless Internet access has just begun to proliferate in many "advanced" nations, and is not terrible advanced in the Third World as of yet. Certainly wireless access, using computers with 802.11 capabilities for example, will doubtless become increasingly popular with terrorists. It may indeed give new meaning to the term "T-Mobile hot spot." Wireless access has rapidly become available in a wide range of public places, such as coffee shops, airports and others. Such locations have all the advantages of the Internet café, as well as the prospect of greater bandwidth and easier file transfer. Anonymous access, paid for on an hourly, daily or some other basis is readily available, and gives the terrorist user immediate access to any account on any commercial service.

Of particular importance to terrorists, operational security is relatively easy, and can be accomplished in a number of ways. First, the simple proliferation of alias accounts and vast number of servers available throughout the world makes "hiding" among the millions of Internet users easy. As any student knows, getting yet another account on yahoo.com, hotmail.com, or any of the other public servers that have proliferated over the past few years takes only a moment and is cost-free. Such accounts can be used for only a few messages and then discarded in favor of yet other accounts in other alias names. Without good and timely collateral intelligence as to the creation of such accounts and names, it is virtually impossible to keep track of their use. Combined with the fact that the actual message content may be either encoded or using cryptograms of some type, the problem becomes even more difficult. The bottom line here is that it has become increasingly easy for terrorists to hide among the millions of Internet users.

Over the last decade there is evidence that various terrorist organizations have set up Internet servers of their own, in a number of foreign countries under what the intelligence services would call commercial cover. Front organizations are used to purchase net bandwidth and register the necessary domain names. These have been easier to detect, and current evidence suggests that the most sensitive of terrorist communications are conducted using alias accounts with the larger commercial services, discussed above. For some time terrorists and others used services known as "third party remailers" which were Internet sites that would forward e-mail anonymously, and presumably thwart the ability to trace any particular message to its source. Currently such remailers have gone out of vogue, and the practice of simply using alias accounts appears to be working as well – or better for this purpose.

It is also possible for terrorists to easily encrypt e-mail and files sent over the Internet, using any number of readily available commercial products. This problem is discussed at greater length in Section 1.2.3 below.

1.2.2   *Finding Terrorist E-Mail*

Much of the foregoing discussion focused on the fact that the Internet and e-mail has quickly emerged as an ideal medium for terrorist communications. This raises the immediate question as to how the intelligence services and law enforcement agencies of nations attempting to combat terrorism can locate and hopefully intercept these communications. This is indeed a major intelligence problem, and an area where limited information is available in the public domain. At a general level, it is possible to note that the intelligence services of the U.S. and most Western nations were exceedingly slow to recognize this as a serious problem at all. Indeed, the potential for criminal or terrorist use of new technologies such as the Internet and cellular telephone was largely ignored and greatly under funded for much of the past decade. What exists now can likely be characterized as too little, very late [19].

While it is possible to fault the Intelligence Community for inadequate attention and insufficient investments in this area, it is also the case that in the long run it may not be possible to accomplish a great deal. There is a fundamental flaw in the American character that says every problem must have a solution, and some corollary that says the solution likely involves technology and money. In this case, it may be close to impossible to find covert terrorist communications sent via e-mail if done "properly." Here properly means that the terrorists learn and adhere to good operations security (OPSEC) procedures. Access to such terrorist communications in the future will likely depend on errors, sloppy procedures, and collateral intelligence information. Examples here include the following:

Informant data on accounts: To the extent that e-mail account names and data are known only to a very few, and are changed with great regularity, it will be difficult to find the accounts and their communications

---

[19] Actual programs in this area are highly sensitive and Government officials are extremely reluctant to discuss them. The recent U.S. House and Senate investigations of the Intelligence Community, as well as the 9/11 Commission Report, have shed a good bit of new light on the extent of these failing.

[20]. Where human sources, or other collateral intelligence sources provide such information, accessing the materials in the account becomes less problematic, although the materials in any given account may be encrypted, causing an additional burden.

Intercept of e-mail traffic in target areas: One technique that has been suggested is to look at the switched packet (IP) traffic being carried over commercial basebands in target areas. Without attempting an extensive technical discussion, it is a process that it not likely to yield significant results in the near term.

1.2.3 *The Impact of Encryption*

There are few technology developments that trouble the world's intelligence services more than the proliferation of commercial encryption products. For decades expert code breakers using the most powerful computers of the time had at least some advantages in dealing with the adversaries of the time. Indeed, for most of recent history encryption has been limited to sensitive government and military communications, and has generally been a commercial failure. There are a few obvious reasons for this. In the "analog era" any high-grade encryption systems were: (a) costly; and, (b) imposed an administrative and logistics burden on the user [21]. Serious encryption required a hardware solution that was both an analog-to-digital converter, as well as a digital encryption device, which was essentially a special purpose computer.

The "digital revolution" discussed above has changed all of this quite radically. With voice, data, and every other type of media now in digital form, and generally in a computer connected to a powerful, high-speed processor, "mixing up the digits" isn't all that much of a problem. All that is really required is a decent encryption algorithm, and these have proliferated as well [22]. At the same time user demands have changed as

---

[20]It would be technically, legally and politically difficult to comb, for example, all accounts on AOL, Yahoo, or Hotmail seeking some that may have been used by terrorists. Where data in the accounts is encrypted, the situation becomes even more difficult. Indeed, there isn't enough electric power in the U.S. to decrypt all the encrypted material on the commercial Internet services today.

[21]Note that the famed World War II German "Enigma" code machine was originally developed by Scherbius for the commercial market. This was a completed failure, going bankrupt in the process, and his machine was taken over by Hitler's SS for military purposes.

[22]For some years the U.S. stuck to a policy that is best described as silly, in trying to solve the problem by restricting export of encryption algorithms that were freely available on the Internet, and the export of commercial software products that were freely available at any software store. If a high school kid can buy it with their allowance, presumable the "bad guys" could do so as well! The net result was that foreign suppliers have come

well. Commercial firms and private citizens alike have become more sophisticated computer users, and are now demanding privacy and security. The increased use of the Internet for commercial transactions, many involving credit cards, and the corresponding proliferation of computer fraud have greatly heightened sensitivity in this area. The use of secure web protocols (e.g., https://) and encrypted file transfers is becoming commonplace. A few critical trends in this area are worthy of note:

- No marginal cost to users: Users of secure web protocols and even security certificates for Internet transactions are not incurring any real cost. While some security certificates need to be purchased on an annual basis, for a truly nominal cost, others are available on the net for free – with a quality equal to that of the types being sold.

- No marginal effort involved: Secure use of the Internet requires little or no additional effort on the part of users. Secure web protocols function automatically, and once security certificates are installed on a computer their use is largely automatic as well The days when security required a dedicated "code clerk" and great inconvenience are long gone.

- Transition to secure applications: While the current generation of commercial software products is not quite there yet, the world is moving rapidly toward an era where encryption will be an integral part of most applications (e.g., word processing, spread sheets, communications, etc.), and files will be saved and transferred in an encrypted form [23]. Security will become seamless process largely transparent to the user.

- Security at multiple levels: In the not too distant future security will actually take place at multiple levels. Files generated by application software will be "saved" on hard drives and other media in an encrypted form; data transferred over the Internet and other local area nets will be encrypted for transmission, using security certificates or other secure protocols; and the Internet basebands themselves will be bulk encrypted. There are no major technical, economic or legal barriers. The era of encrypted everything is rapidly approaching.

For intelligence services and law enforcement agencies seeking to find terror-

---

to dominate this world market.

[23] Just as it is impossible to market a word processing program without a spell checker, for example, future packages will contain file encryption as an essential feature. Consumers will demand it, and it costs the software vendor essentially nothing to add it in the package. Encryption will become seamless and transparent to the user.

ists, spies, criminals and others this is a troublesome future. It is no longer a world where only a small number of encrypted communications existed. Everything will be encrypted. That battle is over. The two remaining questions are:

- Can encrypted communications or files of interest be located at all?
- Will it be possible to decrypt terrorist communications in a timely and cost effective manner so that they are of use?

This is still an area where very little has been published addressing these critical issues in any serious way. It is, however, possible to consider how the available technologies are driving the longer-term answers. First, finding any communications of interest in what is becoming a vast sea of encrypted digital bits and packets will become an ever-daunting task. Using a brute force approach and trying to search a mass of data collected from the network carriers is not likely to be highly productive [24]. At a minimum, it will be necessary to have some "external" indication of the source or recipient of the data. On the other hand, the closer it is possible to get to the source (or recipient) through various means, it is possible to narrow the search considerably. In July 2004, for example, the seizure of several computers used by the al Qaeda in Pakistan made it possible to examine the hard drives for stored messages and files [25].

The answer to the second question is even more problematical. Truly low-grade encryption is a thing of the past. The widespread availability of powerful digital processors and good encryption algorithms has put an end to this. The actual difficulty in "breaking" any encrypted file or message really relates to the specific algorithm and key length used [26]. Even where access is technically possible, the resources required in terms of computer time and manpower are likely to be significant. This alone will severely limit the amount of access. For the world's intelligence services this is clearly not a happy thought, but the golden era of largely unbridled access is over.

---

[24] It is hard to find any good estimates of the actual volume of digital data on the net now, but some attempts put this currently on the order of several exabytes, and increasing rapidly.

[25] This is not the first time that U.S. authorities or their colleagues in friendly states have been able to seize computers belonging to terrorists, drug lords, or other key targets. In several cases these targets have been either foolish or sloppy enough to leave files on these computers in a non-encrypted form. In others, their operators have furnished information during interrogation to enable decryption of the stored files.

[26] In an effort to enable access to encrypted files, the U.S. has attempted to restrict the key length or number of "bits" in any commercial system. This has been largely abortive, and has simply served to drive the commercial security market offshore. Some of the best commercial software, for example, is now being marketed by some former KGB personnel, who have established themselves in Ireland – largely for tax reasons and business incentives provided by the Irish.

1.2.4   *Non E-mail Techniques*

The foregoing discussion has largely focused on e-mail sent over the Internet as a major means of covert communications for terrorists, and indeed, the evidence suggests that it is in fact their preferred method for such communications. There are, however, other techniques for sending such communications and data over the Internet that do no involve the use of e-mail.

Data Embedded in Images (Steganography): One that has been popular for some time has been to embed data in digital images. At the present time there are literally billions of images available on the Internet, hosted on web sites and computers across the planet. This raises the immediate question as to how the intelligence services and law enforcement agencies of nations attempting to combat terrorism can locate and hopefully intercept these communications. There are a number of techniques by which data can be embedded in an image, and is not apparent to anyone viewing the image, but can be retrieved by a knowledgeable recipient. Thus a terrorist or other sender can embed the data on an image posted on the net, or replace a given posted image with one containing the data. The recipient can then download the image from the web, and extract the data, with no apparent link to the sender. This is a more cumbersome approach to "communicating" via the Internet, but provides a significant level of security for the terrorist, and avoids the possibility of detection if used correctly.

Internet "Dead Drops": Another technique for the covert transfer of information using the Internet is for the sender to place a file on a server, using the ftp protocol for example, and then have the recipient remove the file. It is possible to use some unwitting server as the host, and have the file actually remain on the server for only an instant, given some degree of synchronization between the sender and recipient. This is a modern, electronic version of the "dead drop" technique used by intelligence officers for many years [27].

These are only two illustrative ways that the Internet has been used for covert data transfers. Certainly there are others, and more will be developed. It is not a static area, and cleaver computer scientists around the world are actively engaged in this problem. The most important point here is simply that the Internet can be used for covert communications and data transfers in a variety of ways other than simply e-mail, and that such techniques are not highly secret, and more importantly provide a substantial

---

[27]This technique had provided material for several spy novels and movies. In the Cold War days, Moscow's Gorky Park was reportedly a popular location for such activities. One retired intelligence officer has written that in those days it was popular to hide secret messages in hollow rocks and dead rats left in the park. The Internet variant appears to be easier and safer, but much less romantic.

degree of security and freedom from detection.

1.3 Terrorist Access to Information

Moving beyond terrorist use of the Internet for communications, the net has rapidly emerged as the world's greatest source of information, and does not discriminate amongst its users. Indeed, there is ample evidence that terrorists around the globe are regular users of the Internet to obtain information for their various operations.

1.3.1 *Potential Targets for Future Attacks*

In many cases it is far more efficient and less costly for a terrorist organization to obtain information about potential targets from sources available on the Internet. Clearly physical surveillance of any target by terrorist operatives generally involves travel, possible detection and exposure, and certainly significant costs. Using the web, an enormous amount of information can be obtained on a very wide range of targets. Access to this information is easy and in most cases those requesting the information cannot be identified [28].

For many potential targets, a large amount of essential data is available on the net, often including photographs; plans; information on hours of operation; as well as other geographic and operational data of importance. Even where such data may not be sufficient or complete, it may provide the terrorists with a major advantage in simply sorting out potential targets, or reducing greatly the amount of data that needs to be collected by local operatives. Access to the necessary web sites is frequently not restricted and is generally available at no cost to the user. Further, such access is most often granted on an "anonymous" basis with the server site not tracking the user in any realistic way. While many sites do in fact record the IP address of incoming users, it is simply for a sophisticated terrorist to do their web surfing from an Internet connection that cannot readily be traced to them [29].

---

[28]It is possible for excessive data searching to set of some alarms. Recently a group of architecture students seeking data for a project involving a new building at Camp David, the U.S. Presidential retreat, made a sufficiently large number of web searches that it came to the attention of the Secret Service. This is likely a rare case, involving a large number of search requests against a very high value target.

[29]Take, for example, a terrorist who did their web surfing from an Internet café, or the T-Mobile hot spot at a Starbucks! The system dynamically assigns the user an IP address, which is then reassigned to the next user in the shop.

1.3.2   *Logistics for Terrorist Operations*

There is also a substantial amount of evidence that terrorists are increasingly using the Internet for logistics related to their operations. Increasingly aircraft, train and other reservations are made via the Internet. Possibly the most striking example are the terrorists who performed the 9/11 attacks, who obtained their tickets via the Internet [30]. It is a fact of modern life that Internet based web sites are used for schedules, reservations, ticket sales, boarding passes and other aspects of travel. These services provide great efficiencies to both the operators and travelers alike. They also provide a means for terrorists and others to arrange for travel and other logistics, such as package shipping, in a way that provides substantial anonymity. As with e-mail, terrorists can be lost or blend in to the large number of legitimate net users.

The only time terrorists become "visible" is when they are screened at an airport, and this may be only a perfunctory check of their ID. It is in fact the case that false drivers licenses can easily be purchased in major cities, while false passports may be more difficult and costly to obtain do not seem to be beyond the reach of terrorists today.

Since it is highly unlikely that the world will retreat from this mode of operation, and revert to having people use travel agents, airline ticket offices and other old technologies rather than the Internet, the question becomes one of what can really be done, if anything, to detect terrorists using the Internet for such purposes. The "good news" is that all such transactions are in digital form; records are generated; databases exist; credit cards are generally used; and, hopefully law enforcement authorities will have the appropriate access to this data. With this in mind, DARPA, for example, tried to initiate one program to "mine" this data for signs of terrorist activity [31]. Notwithstanding the privacy issues involved, serious technical issues still need to be addressed as to how feasible it will be to detect unlawful or terrorist use of net-based systems for such purposes. Ultimately the results are likely to be mixed, with "sloppy" operations easier to detect than ones where operational security has been well thought out.

---

[30] According to the 9/11 Commission Report, the 9/11 hijackers even enrolled in the American Airlines award mileage program to facilitate their on-line reservations.

[31] At the time the DARPA TIA Program received a significant amount of publicity in the press, much of which was critical and unfavorable to the program, largely on issues related to privacy. This is a valid concern, and one not limited to this program. As databases grow in number and size, the tension between intelligence, law enforcement and the protection of individual rights to privacy will become one of increasing concern.

1.3.3 Technical Data for Terrorist Operations

A matter of increasing concern to the U.S. and others fighting terrorism is the amount of technical data that is freely available on the Internet that is of use to terrorists. While much of the public attention in this area has focused on the extreme end of nuclear technology and weapons systems development, it is also the case that enormous amounts of useful information is also on the Internet in such areas as conventional bomb and other weapons design; chemical weapons; biological weapons; and, other forms of radiological weapons.

Looking first at the worst case of nuclear technology, it is a fact that a considerable amount of sensitive information about the design of nuclear weapons has leaked into the public domain, and can be found on the Internet. Having access to such information, and being able to actually construct a working weapon are, however, worlds apart. Assuming that some terrorist group was able to obtain sufficient weapons-grade nuclear material (enriched uranium or plutonium), the technologies required to actually fabricate a working nuclear weapon are very difficult and complex [32]. There are quite a number of obstacles to overcome here, and the Internet isn't entirely the answer.

Matters are actually more troublesome in the areas of chemical and biological agents, where issues of manufacture are nowhere near as difficult as in the case of nuclear weapons, and the data derived from the Internet can be of substantial use. Included here is information collected via the Web from legitimate technical sources, as well as "rogue" sites and postings by terrorist organizations and others. The use of the web for dissemination of data is considered at greater length in Section 1.4 below.

As a practical matter the weapons most frequently being employed by terrorist organizations at the present time utilize fairly crude technologies. The popular term is "improvised explosive devices" or IEDs, which generally means weapons that have been assembled using parts and explosives obtained from other weapons or shells. By one account, the classic IED is a "155 mm howitzer high explosive round with its detonator screwed off and replaced by a blasting cap and wires" [33]. This is not always the case. Highly sophisticated IEDs have been constructed from arming devices

---

[32] This being said, it is the case that an increasing number of nations have joined the nuclear "club," the most recent probably being North Korea. At this point, the number of North Korean nuclear weapons is unknown, and there have been no reports that the North Koreans have ever tested a weapon and demonstrated the ability to fabricate a working nuclear device.

[33] Interview with Sgt. Maj. Willard Wynn (USA). Wynn continues "the bad guy just hooks these two wires to a battery and bang. It's the big one. It will kill anything in the area."

scavenged from conventional munitions or from easily purchased electronic components, many through Internet sources. The degree of sophistication depends on the ingenuity of the designer, the tools, as well as the materials available. Today IEDs are extremely diverse and may contain any type of firing device or initiator, plus various commercial, military or contrived chemical or explosive fillers. What types of IEDs are used by specific terrorists also is dependant on the local context. The IEDs generally found in Israel and the occupied territories, for example, differ from those found in Iraq. There are far fewer 155 mm howitzer rounds available to the Palestinians, and the form factor does not fit terrorist operations there [34].

1.4   Terrorist Web Sites

As suggested above, the advent of the Internet and the world-wide-web (www) protocol has truly brought about the most significant media revolution in centuries [35]. For the first time in history, anyone with Internet access is easily able to search and immediately access a vast array of information. Information, publications, records and data of every imaginable type is now "on-line" with massive amounts of additional information being added daily. There are in fact no really good estimates of the range and amount of information on the web, although even the most novice of users will quickly find that it is astounding. This being said, a few key points are worth noting:

- Ease of access: All that is required is a relatively simple computer and Internet access. This can be at a home, office, or even a public facility. Research no longer requires going to a library or anywhere else. The logistics burden has been eliminated.
- Zero marginal cost to users: Once one has Internet access, the web can be searched or "surfed" endlessly for no additional cost [36]. The marginal economics here are truly compelling.
- Zero marginal cost to publishers: The marginal economics for con-

---

[34] They are more difficult to smuggle into Israel, and a suicide bomber would not look right trying to walk around with several 155 mm howitzer rounds strapped to their body. Larger devices can be used in car bombs and rockets, which are not as common in Israel as in Iraq. Most of the IEDs found in the Israeli context have been fabricated from "scratch" with salvaged or manufactured explosives and detonators in covert facilities.

[35] It can be noted that critical enabling technology, the hyper-text transfer protocol (http//) - more commonly known as the "web" protocol that has enabled much of this revolution, did not result from a DARPA initiative, but was developed at CERN, the Swiss nuclear research institute.

[36] This is not entirely the case. There are some number of sites that do impose user fees, but these are still relatively limited.

tent providers is also a wonderful story. The costs of establishing a web site have become close to nothing, and once content is put onto a web site it is available to an infinite number of potential users world-wide at no marginal cost [37]. There is no other media that has such scale economies.

- Intelligent users interfaces and search tools: For anyone who engaged in "research" in the old days of books and paper, the tools available for Internet access and search are a miracle. Early net protocols such as the ftp (file transfer protocol) have been replaced by user-friendly web browsers (such as Internet Explorer and Netscape Navigator), while extraordinarily powerful search engines, such as Google, enable Internet users to search the web for relevant materials easily and quickly [38].

These "facts" of modern life have not been lost on terrorist organizations. As with other organizations and group, they have quickly established a large and increasing number of web sites to meet objectives that include dissemination of information; recruitment of personnel; solicitation of funds; and, others.

1.4.1 *Platform for Terrorist Propaganda*

Along with satellite television, the web has turned out to be the preferred medium for dissemination of terrorist "information," including news, propaganda, and other data that the terrorists would like to make available [39]. The actual range of material here is quite broad, and includes written materials, audio transcripts, video clips and other forms of hyper-text. Internet postings of such things ranging from terrorist beheadings of captives to messages from Osama bin Laden have become commonplace. The Hezbollah organization, for example, maintains a multi-lingual web site

---

[37]The actual costs here have really fallen over the last several years, as any student can attest. A web site can be established on virtually any computer connected to the Internet, or hosted on a commercial service for well under ten dollars a month. In practical terms, this amounts to "free." New software tools now enable users to create and maintain web sites with great ease as well.

[38]Interestingly, the web browser began as a relatively small DARPA project called MOSAIC, and the developers quickly moved from this research project at NCSA in Illinois to founding the Netscape Corporation in Palo Alto, CA. Google began in the famed Silicon Valley, and is a great success story as well.

[39]The Lebanese terrorist organization Hezbollah, for example, is a model of modern media use. Over the past decade they have developed al-Manar as a source of information on regional events, broadcast by foreign news media and over the Internet. See Reuven Paz, "Hizballah Considering Satellite Broadcasts," March 22, 2000 at www.ict.org.il and www.hizballah.org.

(www.hizballah.org) that attempts to provide both legitimate "news" as well as other materials for international consumption. It's webmaster, Ali Ayoub has stated "[Hezbollah] will never give up the Internet. We successfully used it in the past when we showed video clips and pictures of the damage caused by Israeli bombings in Lebanon" [40].

Similarly, the Hamas terrorist organization has established its own Internet presence, and are now possibly the most prolific of any such organization in terms of their on-line presence. Their website (www.palestine-info.org) provides both Arabic and English links to a wide range of Hamas resources, including the Hamas charter, official communiqués and statements of its military wing, the Izz al-Din al-Kassam Brigades. Hamas resources are also available through the website of the Muslim Students Association in the U.S.; the Palestinian site of the Islamic Association for Palestine; as well as through the official Hamas website [41].

Other Islamic terrorist organizations dedicated to the destruction of Israel, such as the Palestinian Islamic Jihad (PIJ) have used both the Hezbollah web site as a medium to propagate their beliefs, as well as other regional media, including the al-Jazeera statellite television network and al-Manar. The PIJ also uses an "unofficial" website hosted in Dallas, Texas [42]. The Palestinian Authority (PA) and its primary political party (Fatah), as well as the Al-Aqsa Martyrs Brigade have increasingly used web-based media, such as the online edition of Al-Hayat Al-Jadida for statements in support of their activities, which in turn has been supported by the Palestinian Communications Ministry [43].

1.4.2 *Platform for Terrorist Recruitment and Fundraising*

Closely related to terrorist use of the Internet as a platform for dissemination of news and other propaganda has been the use of this media as a tool for both recruitment and fundraising. In terms of recruitment of additional group members and terrorist operatives the various terrorist sites have not yet featured online application or sign-up forms but have done virtually everything else. Much of the propaganda posted on the terrorist sites is in fact focused on Islamic youth, and potential recruits. Israelis, Jews and their supporters are shown in the worst possible light, and frequently in terms of outrageous falsehoods, while the acts of Islamic martyrs are por-

---

[40] Janes Intelligence Review, November 2001. In September 2000 a group of Israeli hackers attacked six websites of the Hezbollah and Hamas organizations inside Lebanon. Subsequently Hezbollah established a number of alternative sites to avoid future disruptions.

[41] See www.web3way.com.

[42] Ibid.

[43] See www.pmw.org.il.

trayed in the most heroic terms. No research or statistics are yet available with respect to how effective the Internet has been as a terrorist recruiting tool, but there is little doubt that it has been significant.

Hezbollah, Hamas, PIJ and other Middle Eastern terrorist organizations have all used the Internet in a variety of ways to raise funds. These range from the transfer of cash by electronic couriers to legitimate bank accounts then used by the terrorists, to financing of a wide range of front organizations. Included here are Islamic charities, professional associations, and similar institutions for supposed social and educational projects, hospitals, orphanages and other humanitarian initiatives [44]. Contributions to these organizations and causes are generally transferred by legitimate, electronic means to bank accounts in the U.S., Europe and the Middle East. Hezbollah, for example, raises money in the U.S. through the website of the Islamic Resistance Support Association, where users are given the opportunity to fund operations against the "Zionist Enemy" [45]. Likewise, the Hamas-affiliated Holy Land Foundation for Relief and Development permitted visitors to its site to make donations with either credit cards or through electronic transfers, until this site was shut down by the U.S. Government in 2002.

While some sites are in fact closed, as indicated above, others dedicated to assisting these terrorist groups in an ever-broader range of ways emerge, and frequently in places beyond the reach of the U.S. and other friendly governments [46]. This leads to some fundamental questions, namely can or should the U.S. continue to try and stop such operations? The debate in this area is far from over. Since most web content is free speech, protected by the First Amendment, regardless of how offensive it might be, there are serious Constitutional issues involved. Policy and actions in this new area are still in a state of evolution. Aside from the legal issues, is the real question of how able the U.S. and its allies in the war on terrorism are to shut these sites down on any permanent basis. If the models of Internet pornography and gambling are any indication, the answer is not very encouraging. Terrorist organizations have repeatedly demonstrated their ability to move websites to alternate servers and locations, generally outside the U.S. or any other potentially cooperative nations. At best, such efforts to impede terrorist web operations may prove to be a relatively short-term annoyance and not a permanent solution.

---

[44]See Rachael Ehrenfeld, Funding Evil: How Terrorism is Financed – and How to Stop It. (Chicago, Bonus Books, 2003). See also, Reuven Paz, "Targeting Terrorist Financing in the Middle East," October 23, 2000 at www.ict.org.il.

[45]See www.moqawama.net.

[46]Note, for example, the emergence of the new site stopamerica.org following the 9/11 attacks on the U.S., whose administrator has since been indicted as a possible al-Qaeda operative.

1.5 Terrorists and Cyber-Terrorism

Topping the list of possible terrorist abuses of the Internet is the potential for actual attacks on the network itself, or "cyber-terrorism." There is currently significant debate over the real threat from cyber-terrorism, particularly from those viewed as the most serious terrorist groups. There are writers on both sides of this issue, although it is unfortunate that many of those involved in the debate, including government officials, military personnel as well as journalists have limited or no real technical expertise and are commenting on matters they simply do not understand. In part the discussion arises because some people see the two relatively disjoint phenomena (terrorism and cybernetics) and think they must logically intersect at some point [47]. Leaving aside the Hezbollah and al Qaeda for a moment, it is possible to consider the sources of cyber-attacks this far:

- Hackers: To date, the vast majority of all cyber attacks have come from "hackers" of several types. These range from bored high-school kids to those depicted in the film The Matrix. In most cases hackers are best described as malicious, but not actually terrorists. They are not seeking either money or the end of the U.S. (or Israeli) government. For a number of reasons they just get perverse pleasure from annoying others.
- Criminals: Since commerce, banks etc. have increasingly moved to computers and networks, it is only natural that criminals have moved to this venue as well. Since a group of Russian cyber criminals attacked New York's City Bank several years ago, commercial firms have gotten a great deal more interested in protecting their systems from criminal penetration.
- Disgruntled employees: Statistically, by far the largest number of problems and attacks on computer systems still come from former employees (e.g., system administrators) who are angry with their employers, not the nation. In most cases these are current or former "insiders" with at least some technical skills, and more importantly people who still had such critical data as administrative passwords and access to the systems they were attacking [48].

---

[47] See Abraham R. Wagner, "Cyber-Terrorism, Evolution and Trends: Relax Chicken Little, The Sky Isn't Falling, or Get a Grip on Reality." ICT Post Modern Terrorism, Trends, Scenarios and Future Threats, 2003.

[48] Several studies have all pointed to the fact that many firms and organizations routinely fail to change administrative passwords when personnel changes take place. These same organizations that are religious about collecting keys and badges leave their computer "doors" wide open.

Thus far there has really been scant evidence of any significant effort on the part of a major terrorist group to attack the Internet or computers supporting network operations. Further, investigations have failed to turn up a serious technology base or sophisticated development program in this area among any terrorist group that can even rival the average high school student in America. The U.S. and its allies have located and captured a number of individual terrorist operatives with computer skills in varying degrees, but these have generally been operatives supporting terrorist operations, and not involved in network attacks [49]. U.S. intelligence, military and law enforcement officer have captured computers and hardware from all sorts of terrorists worldwide, and the conclusion one can draw is that they are users of the Internet and not attackers of the Internet. This is not to say the situation would not change, but these are the data that exist to date.

There is also mixed evidence as to how serious this threat is, even from experienced attackers. In a 1998 U.S. Department of Defense, exercise called "ELIGIBLE RECEIVER" a "Red Team" of some 35 computer experts from the National Security Agency were given three months to plan and execute an electronic attack on DoD information systems and on elements of the national infrastructure that support DoD [50]. Using only public Internet access and commonly available hardware and software, the Red Team demonstrated that it could untraceably "bring down" the telecommunications system that is the backbone of DoD command and control, as well as a major portion of national electric power grids and 911 systems. Although they only gained "root access" to 36 of the 40,000 Pentagon network servers they interrogated, this was assessed to be enough to have prevented the command and control system from operating effectively to support a deployment.

Evidence like this must be viewed in perspective. First, ELIGIBLE RECEIVER was undertaken some five years ago – at least two net generations past. Second, almost three-dozen NSA technical experts were employed – a resource no terrorist group is likely to have access to. Finally, this group only gained access to a minute fraction of the DoD computers interrogated, and the vulnerabilities that permitted this type of root access have long since been eliminated.

More recently a 2002 exercise held at the U.S. Naval War College called "DIGITAL PEARL HARBOR" using a group of outside experts concluded

---

[49] One good example is the July 2004 capture of an al Qaeda operative in Pakistan who was operating several Internet servers, and transferring files brought to him on disk from Osama bin Laden to the servers for transmission.

[50] Speech by John Hamre before the Council on Foreign Relations, New York, 1998. At the time Hamre was the Deputy Secretary of Defense.

that a terrorist cyber-attack was possible, but would require a 200-million investment and five years to accomplish. Again these were U.S, experts possibly applying Defense Department concepts of program management and funding. Presumably a terrorist organization could undertake a less costly program, but it still suggests the magnitude of the problem for any terrorist group [51].

---

[51] Recall that al Qaeda conducted the entire September 9/11 operation for less than $300,000$. The U.S. DoD would likely spend more on a feasibility study for a similar operation, let alone the costs of the operation itself.

Bibliography

Abbey, A.D. (2004). Virtual Jihad, *Jerusalem Post*, May 6.

Allen, P.D. and Demchak, C. (2003). The Palestinian-Israeli Cyberwar, *Military Review*, March-April.

Cordesman, A.H. (2002). Terrorism, Asymmetric Warfare and Weapons of Mass Destruction: Defending the U.S. Homeland, *Westport, CT: CSIS/Praeger*.

Cyber Attacks During the War on Terrorism: A Predictive Analysis, *Hanover, NH: Institute for Security Technology Studies*, Dartmouth College, 2001.

Ehrenfeld, R. (2004). Islamist Terrorism on America's Internet, www.FrontPageMagazine.com, September 8.

Elliott, J.E. (2002). Cyber Terrorism: A Threat to National Security, *Carlisle Barracks, PA: Army War College*, April 9.

Freiberger, P. and Swaine, M. (2000). Fire in the Valley: The Making of the Personal Computer (2nd Edition), *New York: McGraw-Hill*.

Ganor, B. (2002). Terror as a Strategy of Psychological Warfare, www.ict.org.il, July 15.

Gellman, B. (2002). Cyber-Attacks by Al Qaeda Feared, *Washington Post*, June 27.

Gershwin, L.K. (2001). Cyber Threat Trends and US Network Security, www.cia.gov/cia/public_affairs/speeches/gershwin_speech_062., June 21.

Kahn, D. (1996). The Codebreakers, *New York: Scribner*.

Karmon, E. (2001). The Role of Intelligence in the Fight Against Terrorism, www.ict.org.il, February 26.

Maariv, October 22, 2003

Sageman, M. (2004). Understanding Terror Networks, *Philadelphia, University of Pennsylvania Press*.

Sofaer, A.D. and Seymour E.G. (eds.) (1999). The Transnational Dimension of Cyber Crime and Terrorism, *Stanford, CA: Hoover Institution/Stanford University Press*.

Singh, S. (1999). The Code Book: The Evolution of Secrecy from Mary Queen of Scots to Quantum Cryptography, *New York: Doubleday*.

The 9/11 Commission Report: Final Report of the National Commission on Terrorist Attacks on the Unites States, *New York: W.W. Norton & Co.*,

2004.

Wagner, A. R. (2003). Cyber-Terrorism, Evolution and Trends: Relax Chicken Little, The Sky Isn't Falling, or Get a Grip on Reality, *ICT Post, Modern Terrorism, Trends, Scenarios and Future Threats*.

Wagner, A. R. (2004). Improvised Explosive Devices in Israel and Iraq, *Working Paper for DARPA*, September.

Weimann, G. (2004). How Modern Terrorism Uses the Internet, www.terror.org, United States Institute of Peace Special Report 116, March.

Weimann, G. (2004). OP-ED: Terrorism and the Internet, *Daily Times*, April 30.

Whine, M. (1998). Islamist Organizations on the Internet, www.ict.org.il, April 1.

Wilson, C. (2003). Computer Attack and Cyber Terrorism: Vulnerabilities and Policy Issues for Congress, *Washington: CRS Report for Congress*, October 17.

Yedihot Ahronot, January 1, 1996.

Chapter 2

The Radical Islam and the Cyber Jihad

Shaul Shay

Department of Military History, Israel Defense Forces, Israel
E-mail: shaulshay@hotmail.com

2.1 The New Trends of Terror

The purpose of this paper is to discuss the current concern of the continuing but also evolving threat of radical Islam and terrorism in the "Information Age".

Globalization and the communication era have opened new operational arenas for radical Islamic terror organizations such as Al-Qaeda, Hizballah and Hamas, and have provided them with the opportunity to exploit communication systems, information and funds, as well as supply-services to further their activities.

The Conflict between Al Qaida and the United States is a typical example of an asymmetrical conflict between a terrorist organization or a coalition of terrorist organizations (The Global Jihad) and the one and only superpower and its coalition against terror.

It was Osama Bin Laden who already in 1996 declared war on the United States and then reiterated this declaration with a fatwa (a religious ruling) in February 1998.

Osama bin Laden, the Al Qaida organization, and other radical Islamic organizations have challenged the American superpower and the world order it represents.

Osama bin Laden defined the conflict as part of a historic cultural–religious struggle between Islam and the Jewish Crusader axis whose goal it is to bring Islam down to its knees and conquer its holy lands, [Ranstrop M. (1998)].

Bin Laden's worldview is a combination of his belief in a puritanical ascetic lifestyle as preached by the Wahabists and his extreme radicalism which regards Jihad as the only way to ensure the victory of Islam over its internal and external enemies following the doctrine preached by 'Azam and his students.[1]

Bin Laden subscribes to the idea of a "global Jihad" whose purpose is to unify all of radical Islam in order to bring about his main goal, the destruction of the United States who is seen as the "snake's head" and who according to Bin Laden is the root of all evil in the world.

Bin Laden believes that it is possible to bring the United States to its knees in the same way the Jihad fighters in Afghanistan won a decisive victory against the Soviet superpower following their invasion of an Islamic country, and ultimately destroyed it as an ideological and national entity. Bin Laden does not claim that the local struggles against secular regimes are unimportant, but he does claim that the Islamic movements should concentrate their efforts on destroying the United States which symbolizes western, secular, and anti-Islamic culture.

Bin Laden focuses his struggle on the United States since he believes that its downfall will bring the downfall of all the regimes it supports and protects, among them the secular Islamic regimes and Israel.

Osama Bin Laden is very aware of the asymmetry between his organization and the immense power of the United States. He believes, however, that it is within his power to cause the downfall of the United States. His belief is based on three main principles:

- A deterministic belief in the ultimate victory of Islam over western culture.
- The "precedent" of the Soviet Union' dissolution which radical Islam takes credit for.
- A familiarity with "western culture" – its advantages and abilities but also its weaknesses.

Osama bin Laden does not think that it is within his power to defeat the United States militarily and his response to American superiority is in the cultural realm.

Bin Laden's goal is to shake the pillars of the western value system, of western norms and of western economy. The life and the liberty of the individual is at the center of the western value system and this makes them vulnerable to attacks by a culture whose central value is readiness to totally sacrifice the individual for the good of the Islamic cause and who prefer the afterlife to the reality of the present (the Shahid phenomenon).

Bin Laden is aware that terrorist operations and the threat Al-Qaida

---

[1]'Abdallah 'Azam , of Palestinian origin, was one of the founders of the Global Jihad movement as well as Bin Laden's partner in the Afghani Jihad.

poses to the West force western society to act against some of the basic norms and values that are the basis of their culture. He has become adept at using western technology and democracy to destroy the culture from whence they came.

The strategy employed by Al Qaida is meant to neutralize the relative advantages of the United States and the West who enjoy absolute asymmetry in power and resources.

Three basic elements of this strategy can be identified:

- Carrying out terrorist attack against meaningful and symbolic targets.
- Adoption of suicide attacks as a strategy because of the cultural message and the effectiveness of this type of attack.
- A global battlefield, terrorist infrastructures in every country with the ability to attack at any time and in any place.

The combination of these three elements i.e. suicide bombings against symbolic targets all over the world as well as in the heart of the United States itself constitute Islam's response to the superiority and the asymmetry of the west, in the eyes of Bin Laden.

2.2   Information Terrorism

The global communication system enables a subversive entity such as a terror organization to exploit the various products the system supplies to its users, to maintain a "low-profile signature" within the system and turn the system itself and all its extensions into an arena for their activities and a target for attacks.

In addition to the above concerns, one must also mention the fact that the Internet has led to a change in terrorist communication networks - from strong centralized networks to decentralized networks - due to the nature of Internet. The Internet can also be used for clandestine communications by means of private virtual networks or by sending messages by e-mail or by posting messages on electronic bulletin boards and encrypting them, [Obrien K.A. (2002)].

Tim Thomas coined the term "information terrorism" to describe this exploitation of the internet for terrorist purposes, defining it as in [Thomas (2001)].

- The nexus between criminal information system fraud or abuse, and the physical violence of terrorism.

- The intentional abuse of a digital information system, network, or component toward an end that supports or facilitates a terrorist campaign or action.

Computer attacks are the most often cited example of "the use of force or violence" in the information age because they are the attacks with which everyone has some familiarity.

The Al-Qaeda organization has already proven that despite its worldview, which regards Western culture as Islam's archenemy, it is well acquainted with the potential inherent in Western technology and has learned to exploit this technology for its own needs. Thus, cyberspace has become another arena in which Al-Qaeda and other Islamic organizations wage their holy war (Jihad) against Western culture.

In 2000, former FBI Director Louis Freeh highlighted this issue in a statement to the Senate: "Uncrackable encryption is allowing terrorists – Hamas, Hizballah, Al-Qaeda and others – to communicate their criminal intentions without fear of outside intrusion, [Freeh (2000)].

It is the current belief that Al-Qaeda uses both sophisticated and unsophisticated technologies to coordinate its activities:

The terrorists actively used cyberspace to plan their attacks – they booked airline tickets online, they exchanged hundreds of e-mails, and they used the Internet to learn about the aerial application of pesticides; they also protected their communications by using public computer terminals, anonymous e-mail services, and website encryption to relay information publicly. This modus operandi provided them with total anonymity which was essential for the preparation of these attacks. However, in the aftermath of the attacks the use of cyberspace left an electronic trail which investigators could follow.

As mentioned above cyberspace is an optimal arena for "terrorist entities": they can operate from any location with no need for a territorial base or the development of a permanent and therefore vulnerable infrastructure.

Laptop computers, satellite or cellular telephone and the Internet are the optimal operation and combat arena for this "nomadic entity". Modern terrorists literally have the ability to operate globally. They are no longer limited to employing terrorism as a tactic in a territorially based insurgency. As a result we now witness the emergence of "Non-Territorial Terrorism" – a form of terror that is not confined to a clearly delineated geographical area, [Sloan (1978)].

Thus, a state-like entity dependent upon technology becomes vulnerable and helpless vis-à-vis this "nomadic" element which operates and thrives in virtual space. This is true both of the lone hacker, who can disrupt a national or global system, and of terror cells who manipulate the system for their own malicious purposes, such as accessing targets through cyberspace.

The Information age provides terror organizations such as Al-Qaeda with new opportunities and arenas in which they can operate. The Internet, e-mail and other communication networks sometimes serve as arenas in which terror organization perpetrate their acts and at other times constitute the target themselves.

2.3 The Cyberspace as Battlefield

2.3.1 *Netwars and Networks*

Rand Institute Researchers John Arquilla and David Ronfeldt introduce two new concepts that describe the unique character of the war against modern Islamic terror.

The first concept defines the battle against terrorism as "netwar", [Arquilla *et. al* (1999)]. The researchers define network wars as low-intensity social struggles conducted by networked organizations that operate in small, decentralized units, who can be ready for action at short notice in any place and at any time. The second concept is "networks", which they use to define the elements instigating the struggle in the various networks of cyberspace.

In a broader context Arquilla and Ronfeldt describe netwars as follows: "Netwar refers to an emerging mode of conflict and crime at societal levels, involving measures short of traditional war in which the protagonists are likely to consist of dispersed, small groups who communicate, coordinate and conduct their campaigns in an internetted manner, without a precise central command. Netwar differs from modes of conflict in which the actors prefer formal, standalone, hierarchical organizations, doctrines and strategies, as in past efforts, for example, to build centralized revolutionary movement along Marxist lines".

2.3.2 *The Cyberspace as Cyber-Jihad*

The Information Age has opened up new arenas and has provided the terrorist elements of this day and age with unique "combat means". In the words of radical Islamic organizations this new type of terrorism can be referred to as "**Cyber-Jihad**".

The goal of terror organizations is not to destroy the military capabilities of their adversaries but rather to influence their consciousness and cripple their resolve by undermining their determination and national resilience. Thus, the terrorist aspires to impair and disrupt the lifestyle of target countries, to spread fear and insecurity, and in this way to promote his interests.

To the terrorist, the threat or act of violence is not only a way to generate fear; it is often a strategy or tactic which places heavy emphasis on the use of violence as a form of psychological warfare. As one authority noted, terrorism is a form of psychological operations (PSYOP). Many other characteristics of terrorism are listed by the drafters of competing definitions, but virtually all definitions state, in one way or other, that acts of terrorism are not just act against the immediate victims but also have target audience in mind. Without this additional dimension terrorism would be indistinguishable from other acts of violence, [McEwen (1986)].

The systematic and deliberate use of fear is therefore a central objective of terrorists as they seek to use both threats and violence to create a sense of vulnerability and alter the attitudes and values of the targeted adversary and its population.

These threats can manifest themselves in a number of different ways and are both the means of achieving certain objectives and part of an objective in and of themselves. The threats can have both tactical and strategic impact. At the strategic level, the threats attempt to exploit the fears of the civilian population in order to either weaken their support for the democratic process, undermine the government, or compromise alliances and partnerships between sates; in this sense, the threats have a strong psychological, as well as physical, impact. At the tactical level, the threats can force players to change paths or tactics.

2.3.3   The Trends in the Information Age

The Information Age makes the society and economy of the modern Western state particularly vulnerable because of its great dependency upon communication systems of all kinds for its daily survival.

There are several operation patterns and central threats typical to the Information Age:

Information Combat – This concept consists of many and varied components; Very central to information combat is attacking the adversary's computer systems. In this modern day and age, most of a state's vital systems (infrastructure, economy, security, energy, transportation and others) all rely on computers. Damage to the computers of the various systems may paralyze the systems themselves.

At the present time there are a number of ways to debilitate computer systems, for example, [Shahar].

- Spreading debilitating viruses in computer systems either by introducing the viruses through a remote computer terminal or by planting the viruses in the systems through an "agent".

- "Flooding" sites with electronic mail thus causing their collapse.
- Planting worms in the computer systems (in 1994 the Internet collapsed as a result of this phenomenon).

Both hackers and states have the ability to perpetrate terror attacks of this nature, but terror organizations can learn how, both by training computer experts of their own and by hiring outside hackers, [Time (1995)].

Another part of using information as a weapon is psychological warfare. By its very essence, terror is meant to affect the adversary's consciousness, thus the Information Age provides terror organizations with the appropriate arena and the optimal tools to realize their goals.

Broadcasted Media – The television and radio networks transmit messages and footage from the attack site to the entire world in real time, and provide terrorists with maximum media exposure. The Media, both in its broadcasted and written forms, constitute a conduit through which terrorist are able to transmit messages and wage psychological warfare.

Osama Bin-Laden regularly uses the media to transmit his messages and to wage his psychological war against the United States and the West. In recent years, the Al-Jazeera network has become a major channel for this kind of activity, although Western networks also function as important mouthpieces, [Schweitzer *et. al* (2003)].

Democracy and freedom of speech create an unrestricted communication environment, which the terrorists are able to exploit for their own purposes.

Internet based information and communication systems are an important way to legally gain background information prior to initiating terror attacks. Computerized financial systems enable the transfer of money, providing terror organizations, the financial and logistical aid they require.

Modern communication systems enable terror organizations to communicate with their operatives all over the world in a rapid, efficient and secure way. The use of Internet communication among Al-Qaida operatives is prevalent; their malicious messages are encoded and seem perfectly innocent.

2.4   Conclusion

In summary, the challenges created by the radical Islamic terrorism viewed in the broader context of asymmetric warfare are a manifestation of a profoundly changing conflict environment. While the free world continues to apply the lessons of the past in the fight against terrorism, the new dimensions of terrorist activity created by the interaction of the technological revolution and the transformation of the international arena places a heavy burden upon the free world in its quest to address present and future security concerns.

Furthermore, the challenges created by terrorism require the development of appropriate organizational doctrines and capabilities to combat the threat.

The information age and cyberspace represent an ideal arena for terrorist organizations. The more developed a country becomes, the greater its vulnerability in the area of communications, and the more democratic a country is and the more open its economy, the less restrictions on accessibility and use of these systems. Terrorist attacks against communication systems are relatively easy to perpetrate. The means required for these attacks are not particularly costly, and the perpetrators are difficult to track. The current defense systems provide only a partial response to a wide range of threats, and the development of defensive capabilities is infinitely more expensive than finding ways to damage the system.

The decentralized structure of the organization, the autonomy of the terrorist cells and the way they are spread out around the world (even in western countries) pose a challenge to the United States - a challenge against which conventional army structures and capabilities are irrelevant.

In conclusion, the Asymmetric conflict as conceived by Al Qaida challenges the United States and its allies in a new way, and close international cooperation is required in order to effectively counter the threat.

The challenge of modern terrorism requires deep changes in the way modern western society conceives of conflict management.

Democratic society must protect itself from the elements which threaten its very foundations. Terrorism aspires to bring down western culture and therefore a "defensive democracy" is required, a democracy which is willing to dedicate all its resources and temporarily give up some of its values in order to prevail. Facing the terrorist challenge will sometimes require changes in legislature, such as providing law enforcement agencies with more sweeping powers and allowing authorities to infringe on the privacy of individuals so as to uncover terrorist infrastructure by means of databanks and information at the disposal of the various agencies.

Effectively striking against terrorist funding may require the government to alter some of its financial and banking regulations to allow the authorities access to information concerning various bank accounts. If a terrorist connection is found the authorities must have the ability to freeze or even confiscate the funds.

This is an asymmetrical conflict of a new type – a conflict in which Islamic terror poses a threat to the very existence of the west. The threat alone is enough to inflict significant damage to the foundations of democratic society.

In many ways this is a model of upside down asymmetry in which "the weak's weakness" neutralizes many of the elements which make the strong side strong.

This complicated reality requires conceptual as well as concrete changes in the west, but first and foremost it requires international cooperation, only thus will the challenge be successfully met.

Bibliography

Arquilla, J., Ronfeldt, D. and Zanini, M. (1999). Networks, Netwar and Information Age Terrorism, *Ian O. Lesser, Bruce Hoffman, John Arquilla Brian Jenkhins, David Ronfeldt and Michele Zanini (eds) Countering the new Terrorism, Santa Monica, CA: RAND*

Freeh, L. (2000). FBI chief says cyber Attacks Doubled in a year. http://www.Infowar.com, March 28.

McEwen, M.T. (1986). Psychological Operations Against Terrorism: The Unused Weapon, *J. Military Review*, January, p.62.

Obrien, K.A. (2002). Networks, Netwar and Information — Age Terrorism, *Andrew Tan & Kumar. Ramakrishna (eds), The New Terrorism, Anatomy, Trends and Counter Strategies, Eastern University press, Singapore*, p.86.

Onward Cyber Soldiers, *Time*, **146(8)**, August 21, 1995.

Ranstrop, M. (1998). Interpreting the Broader Context and Meaning of Bin Laden's Fatwa, *J. Studies in Conflict Terrorism*, **21**, October–December.

Schweitzer, Y. and Shay, S. (2003). The Globalization of Terror, The Challenge of Al Qaeda and the Response of the Informational Community Transaction Publishers, New Brunswick, USA, p.220.

Shahar, Y. The Perfect Terror Weapon, *Information Warfare*, www.ict.org.it.

Sloan, S. (1978). The Anatomy of Non-Territorial Terrorism: An Analytical Essay, *Clandestine and Technology Series, Gaithersburg, MD: The International Association of Chiefs of Police*, p.3.

Thomas, T.L. (2001). Deterring Asymmetric Terrorism Threats to Society in the Information Age, http://www.waaf.ru/31.htm, October.

Chapter 3

Using Data Mining Technology for Terrorist Detection on the Web

Mark Last

Department of Information Systems Engineering,
Ben-Gurion University of the Negev, Beer-Sheva, Israel
E-mail: mlast@bgu.ac.il

3.1 Introduction: Who is Hiding in Cyber Caves?

The evidence of terrorists using the internet as a command and control infrastructure goes back as far as 1997. According to Jane's Foreign Report, "a full range of instructions for terrorist attacks, including maps, photographs, directions, codes and even technical details of how to use the bombs are being transferred through the Internet" [Cyber-terrorism (1997)]. A few years after this report was published, the 9-11 hijackers have indeed used the internet to communicate with each other, while staying completely unnoticed by the intelligence agencies [Corbin (2002)]. As the German authorities have discovered after the tragic events of September 2001, the members of the infamous Hamburg Cell have actively used a computer for Internet research on flight schools and other topics of their interest [Com. Rep. (2004)].

The military pressure put on the al-Qaeda leadership in Afganistan after 9/11 has dramatically increased the role of the internet in the infrastructure of the Global Terror Network [Corera (2004)]. In terrorism expert Peter Bergen's words: "They lost their base in Afghanistan, they lost their training camps, they lost a government that allowed them do what they want within a country. Now they're surviving on internet to a large degree. It is really their new base" [Ben-Dov *et. al* (2004)]. Beyond propaganda and ideology, jihadist sites seem to be heavily used for practical training in kidnapping, explosive preparation, and other "core" terrorist activities, which were once taught in Afghan training camps. US Deputy Defense Secretary Paul D. Wolfowitz, in testimony before the House Armed Services Committee recently, called such Web sites "cyber sanctuaries" [Lipton *et. al* (2004)].

Opposite to the common belief, some instructions on future terrorist attacks are aimed at the "broad audience", meaning that terrorists have no reason to conceal them by encryption tools of any kind. Thus, in December 2003 a web site in Arabic published a detailed plan by Bin-Laden associates to force the US and its allies to withdraw from Iraq. The document specifically mentioned the fact that the Spanish government may lose the upcoming elections if Madrid will be hit by terrorist attacks [Walla (2004)]. In March 2004, just shortly before the Election Day in Spain, Madrid was hit by a fierce terrorist attack, which had apparently affected the election results and the subsequent policy of the new Spanish government in Iraq.

Still, the abundance and quality of freely available encryption tools is disturbing. Thus, one can use steganography to hide important textual information inside a digital image or a digital song. Other, less sophisticated means include simple, prearranged code words. Some reports have suggested that Mohammed Atta, suspected of being the leader of the Sept. 11 hijackers, transmitted the following cryptic message to his co-conspirators over the Internet: "The semester begins in three more weeks. We've obtained 19 confirmations for studies in the faculty of law, the faculty of urban planning, the faculty of fine arts, and the faculty of engineering" [Zeller (2004)].

While terrorists are actively using the internet as a communication, intelligence, and propaganda tool, there is no evidence yet of any terrorist organization attempting to carry out a cyber terrorist attack against critical web infrastructures [Holmes (2004)]. However, the possibility of such an attack in the future should not be ignored. With current patch-based approach to computer security, the threats of a costly cyber attack are constantly increasing. One of the main reasons is that some 20 years ago, only well-educated computer experts could understand the inner workings of an operating system and exploit its vulnerabilities. Today, it is possible for a high school student to mount an attack by just downloading automated scripts from the Internet [Khosla (2004)].

What can data mining techniques do to counter these current and future threats of cyber-based terrorism? This chapter is organized as follows. In Section 3.2, we present a comprehensive taxonomy of leading data mining methods and their unique features. Based on this taxonomy, we proceed with defining the main data mining needs and challenges for cyber security and cyber intelligence. Section 3.3 describes a series of evolving data mining techniques that can be efficiently used in cyber warfare. The potential contribution of data mining technology to the counterterrorism effort is summarized in References.

3.2   Data Mining for Countering Terror in Cyberspace

3.2.1   *Taxonomy of Data Mining Methods*

Data mining is recognized as the pivotal technology for combating terrorism and ensuring homeland security [Mena (1999)]. According to [Fayyad *et. al* (1996)], data mining is defined as the core stage of the knowledge discovery in databases (KDD) is "the nontrivial process of identifying valid, novel, potentially useful, and ultimately understandable patterns in data". The KDD process involves, usually, the following stages: data selection, pre-processing, transformation, data mining (induction of useful patterns), and interpretation of results. A pattern is a very general concept, which may refer to a rule, concept, association, link, predictive model, etc. depending on a particular application. The basic expectation of data miners is that patterns, as opposed to incidents of random behavior, repeat themselves and thus can be detected and understood by analyzing the historic data. Some implications of this common phenomenon for detecting terrorist plots and activities in cyber space are discussed in the next sub-section.

As shown in Figure 3.1, two main types of data mining techniques are verification-oriented, where a pre-specified pattern is checked against the available data and discovery-oriented, where the system is looking for new, previously unknown rules and patterns autonomously. The verification-oriented methods include the most common techniques of traditional statistics, like goodness-of-fit test, comparison of means, and analysis of variance (ANOVA). These methods are less associated with data mining than their discovery-oriented counterparts are, since in most real-world situations we are concerned with finding new patterns in large amounts of available data rather than testing known ones.

Srikant, Agrawal, and other researchers have developed a series of automated algorithms for discovering frequent patterns in transaction databases and other types of information repositories (e.g., see [Srikant *et. al* (1996)]). The extracted patterns (association rules) have the form "if event X occurs, then event Y is likely". Events X and Y may represent items bought in a purchase transaction, documents viewed in a user session, medical symptoms of a given patient and many other phenomena recorded in a database over time. Applications of association rules range from basket data analysis to web log mining [Han *et. al* (2001)]. Discovered rules are evaluated by two main parameters: support, which is the probability that a transaction

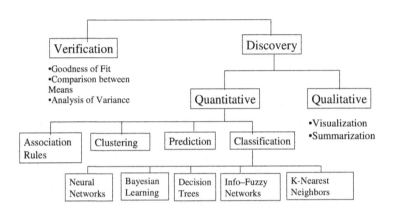

Fig. 3.1   Taxonomy of Main Data Mining Methods

contains both X and Y and confidence, which is the conditional probability that a transaction having X also contains Y. Scalable algorithms, such as Apriori and FP-Tree have been developed for mining association rules in large databases containing millions of multi-item transactions.

Cluster Analysis, or clustering, is a data mining technique aimed at grouping an unorganized data set (e.g., collection of web documents) into clusters (groups) of similar data objects (see [Han *et. al* (2001)] and [Jain *et. al* (1999)]). High quality clusters are characterized by high similarity of their elements to each other along with a low similarity to elements of any other cluster. Clustering applications include marketing, image processing, web mining, and many other areas. One of the most important goals of cluster analysis is to discover hidden patterns, which characterize groups of seemingly unrelated entities (transactions, individuals, documents, etc.). As shown by Chapters 4 and 6 of this volume, clustering of "normal walks of life" can also serve as a basis for the task of anomaly detection: an outlier, which does not belong to any normal cluster, may be an indication of abnormal, potentially malicious behavior.

The task of predictive modeling is to predict unknown values of continuous-valued functions. Typical applications include weather forecasting and financial modeling. Predictive model can only be constructed from a training set of historic records, where the value of the target function is already known. Linear and non-linear regression models have been the most common predictive tool for many years. Regression methods are computationally efficient, but each particular regression method assumes a pre-determined form of functional dependency (e.g., linear) and provides no indication of the existence of other functional dependencies in data.

When the target function has a discrete set of possible values (categories, class labels, etc.), the problems are usually referred to as classification tasks. Some classification techniques of pattern recognition and data mining are based on artificial neural networks (ANNs), which are remarkable for their learning efficiency, but strongly limited in their interpretation capabilities [Mitchell (1997)]. Conditional dependency and independence relations between multiple variables, or causes, are directly treated by Bayesian learning methods. The most straightforward, and often the most efficient, Bayesian learning method is the Naive Bayes Classifier (NBC), which is based on the simplistic assumption that the causes are conditionally independent given the effect. If no conditional independence between variables, given the target attribute, can be pre-assumed, one can use a decision-tree induction algorithm such as $C4.5$ [Quinlan (1993)]. The decision tree model is the most general method of representing non-linear functional relationships and it is widely used in health care, banking, and other domains. A decision tree can easily incorporate both discrete and continuous features, and its branches can be interpreted as if then rules of varying complexity. Decision tree is also a highly scalable classification tool, since it requires a minimal computational effort to find a unique prediction for each new case (record) in the database by traversing a decision tree structure. To induce a compact decision-tree model with a minimum number of predictive features, the Info-Fuzzy Network (IFN) algorithm can be applied [Last *et. al* (2004); Maimon *et. al* (2000)].

Instead of looking for some global patterns in data, one may be interested in just classifying new objects based on the stored data items. This effectively means that each instance stored in a database becomes a local "model" in its own right. Such "lazy" approach may lead to higher classification accuracy in situations, where no global model is needed and classification speed is not of highest importance. K-Nearest Neighbor (k-NN) algorithm is the most popular method of instance-based learning [Mitchell (1997)].

State-of-the-art computer graphics can be used to create visual images, which aid in the understanding of complex, often massive representations of data [Han *et. al* (2001)]. Visual data mining is defined as the process of discovering implicit but useful knowledge from large data sets using visualization techniques. Since "a picture is worth a thousand words", the human eye can identify patterns, trends, structure, irregularities, and relationships among data much faster in a representative landscape than in a spreadsheet. Scatter plots, boxplots, and frequency histograms are examples of techniques used by descriptive data mining. The main limitation of the visual data analysis is its purely subjective approach, since the same data representation may be interpreted in different, sometimes misleading, ways. In [Last *et. al* (1999)], the concepts of Fuzzy Set Theory are used to automate the process of human perception based on pre-defined objective criteria. The automated tasks of data visualization include comparison of frequency histograms, evaluating reliability of database variables, and detecting outliers in noisy data.

3.2.2   *Data Mining Needs and Challenges for Cyber Security and Cyber Intelligence*

Most terrorists do not act in isolation and terrorist networks have many characteristics of organized and semi-organized crime. This is why terrorist plots and activities always leave an "information signature", which in no way is easy to detect, in the form of communications, computer sessions, financial transactions, travel itineraries, etc [Popp *et. al* (2004)]. Relationships between organizations, individuals, events, locations, etc. are the subject of link analysis, which is the process of building up networks of interconnected objects in order to explore patterns and trends. The basic question asked by link analysis software is "Who knows whom, and when and where have they been in contact?" Link analysis is mainly a descriptive tool for visual representation of relationships between a limited set of objects. Applying link analysis to large collections of unstructured web documents is described in sub-section 3.3.1 below.

Due to the extent of Internet usage by terrorist organizations (see Chapters 1 and 2 of this volume in addition to Section 3.1 above), the cyber space can be a valuable source of information on their current activities and intentions. However, the World Wide Web is a distributed information source that contains highly non-homogeneous data organized according to different human association models and value schemes [Mladenic (1999)]. Moreover, no search engine can guarantee 100% coverage and currency of all existing web documents. On the other hand, the CPU power of many computers is not used to its full capacity most of the time. All this makes web-crawling with meta-search agents the most promising approach to active exploration of the infinite web content. Sub-section 3.3.2 below covers the state-of-the-art of the search agent technology.

The content of most web sites is subject to continuous changes over time. Timely discovery of an ongoing trend in certain web content may contribute to early detection of some important changes in the online and the offline behavior of the monitored organization. Moreover, the characteristics of the trend itself (e.g., an increasing or a decreasing occurrence of certain key phrases) may represent the nature of these changes. Several evolving techniques for trend discovery in web documents are described in sub-section 3.3.3 below.

Traditional data mining algorithms are based on the assumption that the training data set is a random sample drawn from a stationary distribution. In contrast, the patterns presenting in most real-world data streams may change drastically over time. Moreover, there is an exponential growth in the amount of data collected by modern information systems, especially in the area of communications intelligence (COMINT). Eventually, the rate of data arrival and change may significantly exceed the learning rate of the data mining system, making the results discovered by the complete data mining process hardly relevant to the future data. In sub-section 3.3.4 below, we describe a series of real-time data mining algorithms, aimed at optimizing the classification performance under a dynamic arrival rate of non-stationary data.

In the 21st century, a major part of people's lives in the civilized world is controlled by software-based systems, often accessible and even controlled from the cyber space. Consequently, there is a common opinion among the security experts that a terrorist attack using cyber methods is just a matter of time. Discovering the actual cause of a software failure may be extremely difficult, like in the case of the Northeast power blackout in the US, since our software systems are still far from being 100% reliable for a variety of reasons. Still, the effects of a software programming error, the effects of a user mistake or the effects of someone deliberately changing the system behavior are all quite similar. A novel, DM-based methodology for automated testing of complex software systems is covered by sub-section 3.3.5.

3.3 Key Techniques of Cyber Warfare

3.3.1 *Link Analysis*

Link analysis is defined in [Ben-Dov *et. al* (2004)] as "the process of building up networks of interconnected objects in order to explore patterns and trends". Like many other data mining techniques, link-analysis tools can only operate on structured data. To discover links in unstructured text documents, such as web pages, information extraction (IE) tool are needed. Ben-Dov et al. [Ben-Dov *et. al* (2004)] propose two alternative techniques for creating links out of unstructured documents: co-occurrence link and semantic link.

Two entities (phrases) co-occur within the same lexical unit if they both are contained within that unit [Feldman *et. al* (2002)]. The most common lexical unit is the sentence unit, but a paragraph or an entire document may also be considered as lexical units. The co-occurrence approach ignores the syntactic or the semantic role of each phrase. Co-occurrence links are usually visualized on a relationship graph by varying the color of the connecting edges as a function of the co-occurrence frequency. The nodes on that graph represent the phrases of interest for the user such as names of some important people (e.g., terrorist suspects). Consequently, the user is able to identify previously unknown and potentially hidden links between people, organizations, events, etc. Thus, an anti-terror example from [Ben-Dov *et. al* (2004)] shows how link analysis can detect an indirect connection between Osama Bin-Laden and the Pope. The person linking between the two is Ramzi Yousef, a convicted terrorist closely related to Bin-Laden and Al-Qaeda, who also tried to assassinate John Paul II during his visit to Philippines in 1995.

Discovery of semantic links is based on noun phrase and verb identification in each sentence. According to [Ben-Dov *et. al* (2004)] and [Feldman *et. al* (2002)], the link extraction process includes the following five layers:

- Layer 0 - part of speech (POS) tagger. Assigning POS tags (noun, proper noun, verb, etc.) to each word.
- Layer 1 - noun phrase and verb phrase grouper. For nouns, it means grouping together the head noun with its left modifiers and, for verbs, connecting a main verb with its auxiliaries (e.g., 'does not').
- Layer 2 - verb and noun pattern extractor. Extracting larger verb and noun phrases, based on semantic requirements.
- Layer 3 - named entity recognizer. Identifying domain-specific entities such as individuals, companies, geographical locations etc.
- Layer 4 - template ('relationship') extractor. Rule-based extraction of patterns at a full sentence or phrase level, using the components found at previous layers. Such templates are usually based on domain-specific subject-verb-object structures.

In [Ben-Dov *et. al* (2004)], the two link-analysis techniques (co-occurrence link and semantic link) are compared using the following evaluation criteria: precision (percentage of correct links out of links retrieved) and recall (percentage of correct links out of total links in the whole document collection). The results of three experiments, each related to a relationship between two specific persons in the news, show that semantic links produce more focused results with significantly higher precision rates than co-occurrence links. The main advantages of the "naïve" co-occurrence approach are a smaller pre-processing effort required and a nearly complete coverage of all co-occurrences. The recall of exactly 100% was not reached in [Ben-Dov *et. al* (2004)] due to anaphors of persons' names (he, she, etc.) that could not be resolved by the information extraction system.

3.3.2 *Information Agents*

An intelligent software agent is an autonomous program designed to perform a human-like function over a network or the Internet. Specifically, information agents are responsible for filtering and organizing unrelated and scattered data such as large amounts of unstructured web documents. Agents represent a key technology to homeland security due to their capability to monitor multiple diverse locations, communicate their findings asynchronously, collaborate with each other, analyze conditions, issue real-time alerts, and profile possible threats [Mena (1999)].

For ordinary users, internet search engines serve as the primary means of information search on the web. A list of major search engines can be found at [Sullivan (2004)]. The source of search engines power, as well as their main limitation, is a huge index of web pages. The index is an inverted file (repository of key words and pages that contain them), which is constantly updated by crawlers that attempt to cover every document in cyber space. While providing minimal response times to millions of simultaneous queries, an index is neither an accurate, nor a complete representation of the actual web [Menczer *et. al* (1999)]. It may take between a few days and a few weeks before a new or changed document is updated in an index of some search engines, while other engines may ignore it forever. An opposite problem is of a search engine continuing to point to a moved or deleted page. Consequently, the results returned by search engines suffer from low recall (percentage of relevant pages that are retrieved) along with even lower precision (percentage of retrieved pages that are relevant). Meta-search engines (see [Sullivan (2004)]) may improve the recall, but only at the expense of reduced precision. Thus, manual browsing of engines' hit lists is hardly the most practical way to find brief announcements posted by terrorist organizations for several days or even hours and often intended to be read by a very limited number of web users. By the time, a search engine will access the corresponding page to update its index, the vital information may be gone and even the site itself may go down re-appear under a new web address some time later.

Autonomous information agents is the evolving solution to the problem of inaccurate and incomplete search indexes [Cesarano *et. al* (2003); Klusch (2001); Menczer *et. al* (1999); Mladenic (1999); Mladenic (1996);

Pant *et. al* (2004); Yu *et. al* (2000)]. The basic idea of the search agent technology is to imitate the behavior of an expert user by submitting a query to several search engines in parallel, determining automatically the relevancy of retrieved pages, and then following the most promising links from those pages. The process goes on using the links on the new pages until the agent resources are exhausted, there are no more pages to browse, or the system objectives are reached [Pant *et. al* (2004)].

Intelligent information agents can be classified in several ways [Klusch (2001)]. They can be either cooperative or non-cooperative with each other. Agent functionality is usually based on a set of information processing rules that may be explicitly specified by the user, acquired by a knowledge engineer, or induced by data mining algorithms. Most popular data mining techniques used by information agent systems include artificial neural networks, genetic algorithms, reinforcement learning, and case-based reasoning. Agents can also be adaptive, i.e. continue to learn from the environment and change their behavior accordingly. According to [Klusch (2001)], any information agent should possess the following key capabilities: access to heterogeneous sites and resources on the web (from static pages to web-based applications), retrieving and filtering data from any kind of digital medium (including documents written in any language and multimedia information), processing of ontological knowledge (e.g., expressed by semantic networks), and information visualization.

An agent-based system called InfoSpiders is described in [Menczer *et. al* (1999)]. Initially, the user provides a keyword query and a list of links returned by a search engine in response to the query. Each autonomous agent is positioned at one of the retrieved documents and given an initial amount of "energy". The user also provides the maximum number of pages to be visited by all agents collectively. An agent obtains a feedback from each visited page in terms of energy reward or loss as a function of page relevancy to the user's topic of interest. The agents use a so-called Q-learning algorithm (see [Mitchell (1997)]) to predict the best links to follow based on these reinforcement signals. The relevance of each outgoing link in a given document is estimated by a neural net, where inputs represent the distances of discriminating keywords from that link. This resembles an earlier system called WebWatcher [Mladenic (1996)], where the interestingness of a link is determined from the underlined words in the hyperlink itself, words in the hyperlink neighborhood, and words in preceding headings.

A multi-agent prototype system of learning text-based agents is presented in [Yu *et. al* (2000)]. The system, called EVA, keeps a repository of "user profiles" (topics of interest). Each profile is characterized by a user query (processed by a natural language processor) and a list of starting URLs that may be provided by the user or based on a domain-specific hierarchy of subject categories (such as Yahoo! Directory). The system creates an agent leader for each user profile. The agent leader generates a team of information agents that are equipped with artificial neural networks aimed at making "relevant / non-relevant" decisions on each retrieved page. In [Yu *et. al* (2000)], the neural networks of search agents are pre-trained on Yahoo! Directory links in specific categories. Each neural network can be further trained on user/manual or automatic feedback expressing the relevance of each retrieved document. Thus, EVA is an adaptive agent system. The population of agents is periodically evolved using a neuro-genetic algorithm that selects the best terms discriminating between relevant and non-relevant documents. The EVA agents are spawned in parallel in response to a user query and each agent operates as a multi-threaded process. The "producer" thread uses the breadth-first search strategy to traverse all hyperlinks at a given web page, while the "consumer" thread is analyzing the retrieved web page to determine its relevance to the user's topic of interest.

A recent paper by Cesarano et al. [Cesarano *et. al* (2003)] presents a prototype of an ontology-based system for information retrieval on the web. The system input includes a user query, the maximum depth to be reached by the information agents ("Web Spiders"), the language of pages to be found, and the context of the related topic in the form of a semantic network. The document pre-processor extracts for each HTML page the title, the content, the description (if provided), and the keywords (if provided). The ontology about the domain of interest is characterized by a set of relevant concepts (terms) and their relationships. The weight associated with a link between two concepts represents the strength of their semantic relationship. The global relevance grade of a given page is computed as a combination of a syntactic grade (based on page ranking by a search engine), a semantic-syntactic grade (based on the presence of domain-related words), and a semantic grade (based on the domain-specific semantic network). The relative weight of each grade is determined empirically.

To sum-up this partial list of research multi-agent systems, the area of text-based information agents seems to be close to its maturity and we should see the first commercial systems implementing this technology within the next few years if not earlier. However, one may argue that artificial neural networks are not necessarily the best data mining method for web agent learning, since their design and training are highly non-trivial processes [Mitchell (1997)]. In fact, training of any standard classification algorithm may be problematic due to an extremely small amount of "positive" examples (pages related to a specific topic such as terrorism) vs. a glut of irrelevant documents on all other topics in the world. General-purpose classification algorithms are designed to learn from relatively balanced data. This means that for topic-oriented information agents one needs a special class of classification algorithms that are sensitive to detection of extremely rare classes (such as the cost-sensitive algorithm presented in [Provost *et. al* (2001)]).

3.3.3   *Trend Discovery*

Most web content mining techniques assume a static nature of the web content. This approach is inadequate for long-term monitoring of the web traffic, since both the users interests and the content of most web sites are subject to continuous changes over time. Timely detection of an ongoing trend in certain web content may trigger periodic re-training of the data-mining algorithm. In addition, the characteristics of the trend itself (e.g., an increased occurrence of certain key phrases) may indicate some important changes in the online behavior of the monitored web site and its publishers.

Recently, several methods have been proposed for change and trend detection in dynamic web content (see [Chang *et. al* (2001)]). All these methods deal with time-stamped documents or versions of the same document downloaded from the web, where a trend can be recognized by a change in frequency of certain topics over a period of time. The topics are usually associated with some key phrases or noun-phases occurring in the documents. A k-phrase is defined as an iterated list of phrases with k levels of nesting. According to [Chang *et. al* (2001)], the algorithm used to discover trends in a collection of time-stamped documents has three major phases: identification of frequent phrases, generating histories of phrases, and finding patterns that match a specified trend.

Defining a trend (such as "upwards", "downwards", etc.) is a truly subjective and user-dependent task. Lent et al. [Lent *et. al* (1997)] propose a Shape Definition Language (SDL), which allows the users to specify queries with respect to their trends of interest in a text database. A "shape" is defined as a sequence of time intervals and their associated slopes. Actual trends are discovered by scanning a set of key phrases and identifying those that match the given shape query. Each keyphrase frequency is measured by the number of documents that contain the phrase. Trends are the k-phrases selected by the shape query with the additional information of the periods where the trend is supported. The trend discovery method of [Lent *et. al* (1997)] has been successfully applied to the US Patent Database.

A trend discovery system for mining dynamic content of news web sites is presented in [Mendez-Torreblanca *et. al* (2002)]. The monitored web pages are downloaded by a dynamic crawler (web information agent) that is activated periodically, e.g., on a daily basis. The pre-processing module of this system implements POS (part-of-speech) tagging to identify the most frequent noun strings that are used for constructing a list of topics. Frequency of a topic is calculated as the number of the news reports mentioning the topic in a given period. Trend analysis is performed by comparing the probability distributions of the news topics in two consecutive periods (e.g., weeks). Individual topics changes are calculated as the absolute differences between the probabilities of topic occurrence. First, the overall change between the two periods is calculated. In case of a significant overall change, the proposed method identifies the main change factors (news topics) along with the "stable" topics that maintain the same level of importance in both periods.

The problem of detecting a change in two consecutive versions of the same web page is discussed by Jatowt and Ishizuka [Jatowt *et. al* (2004)]. This problem is directly related to the area of Topic Detection and Tracking (TDT), which is focused on recognition and classification of events from online news streams. Two types of textual changes are considered: an insertion and a deletion. Single words and bi-grams are used as selected features (terms). Maximum score is assigned to terms, which are inserted or deleted from a high number of documents within a relatively short period of time.

Characterizing a change in topic frequency between two consecutive periods is an extremely subjective task, which is much easier for a human eye comparing frequency histograms of the two periods than for numeric statistical techniques. The human conclusions tend to bear some amount of vagueness and are much easier to be described by words (e.g., "most", "significantly", etc.) than by some strict mathematical terms. People are also trying to rely on the existing expert knowledge, which is linguistic and imprecise in its nature. Thus, evaluating the difference between frequencies of a given topic can be seen as a particular case of approximate (or fuzzy) reasoning (see [Kandel *et. al* (1996)]). Consequently, we can use the fuzzy set theory to model this process. In [Last *et. al* (2002)], the difference between proportions (relative frequencies) is defined as a linguistic variable, which can take two values: bigger and smaller, each being a fuzzy set. If there is an increase in topic frequency between the two periods (a topic is emerging), the membership grade of the difference between proportions in the bigger fuzzy set will be close to 1 and its membership in the smaller fuzzy set will be close to 0. An opposite situation will occur when a topic is disappearing, i.e., there is a decrease in its relative frequency.

3.3.4 *Real-Time Data Mining*

We are witnessing an exponential growth in the amount of data recorded by modern computer systems, especially in the area of web traffic. The reported rates include the maximum amount of 17,400 Web page requests per minute at a single university campus, 500, 000 transactions recorded during less than one day by the Lycos search engine, and tens of millions of queries sent every day to Yahoo! Search [Last (2002)]. Eavesdropping on communication lines of a middle-size US Internet Service Provider, such as EarthLink with about 5.2 million subscribers, would require simultaneous processing of more than 9, 000 pages per second. One of the main difficulties in mining such massive data streams is to cope with the changing data concept. The online behavior of web users may change over weeks, days and even minutes, at times drastically. This change, also known as concept drift [Widmer *et. al* (1996)], causes the data-mining model generated from past data, to become less accurate in the classification of new data. Moreover, the rate of data arrival and change may significantly exceed the learning rate of the data mining system, making the results discovered by the conventional data mining process hardly relevant to the future data [Last (2002)].

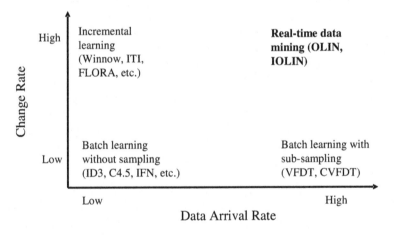

Fig. 3.2   Mining Continuous Data Streams

The common approach of batch learning algorithms (ID3, C4.5, IFN, etc.) is to store and mine the entire set of training examples under the assumption that the concept is nearly stable and the new data arrives at a relatively low rate (see Figure 3.2). Methods for mining continuous streams of data are known as incremental (online) learning algorithms. The pure incremental learning methods take into account every new instance that arrives. Widmer & Kubat [Widmer *et. al* (1996)] have described a series of purely incremental learning algorithms that flexibly react to concept drift and can take advantage of situations where context repeats itself. Their series of algorithms is based on a framework called FLORA, which maintains a dynamically adjustable window during the learning process. Whenever a concept drift seems to occur (a drop in predictive accuracy) the window shrinks (forgets old instances) and when the concept seems to be stable the window is kept fixed. Otherwise, the window keeps growing until the concept becomes stable. FLORA is an ideal method to cope with abrupt and drastic changes in the underlying concept, but it suffers from a poor scalability, since it updates the classification model with every example added to or removed from the training window.

Domingos & Hulten [Domingos *et. al* (2000)] have proposed the VFDT (Very Fast Decision Trees learner) system in order to overcome the longer training time issue of the pure incremental algorithms. The VFDT system is using a decision tree learning method, which builds the trees based on sub-sampling of a stationary data stream. To deal with changing data streams, Domingos & Hulten [Domingos *et. al* (2001)] have proposed an improvement to the VFDT algorithm which is called CVFDT (Concept-adapting Very Fast Decision Tree learner). CVFDT applies the VFDT algorithm to a sliding window of a fixed size and builds the model in an incremental manner instead of building it from scratch whenever a new set of examples arrives. CVFDT grows alternate sub-trees at its internal nodes and modifies the model when the alternate sub-tree becomes more accurate than the original one.

In [Last (2002)], we have introduced an online classification system that uses an info-fuzzy network (IFN) as a classification model. The system called OLIN (On Line Information Network) gets a continuous stream of non-stationary data and builds a network based on a sliding window of the latest examples. OLIN detects a concept drift (an unexpected rise in the classification error rate) and dynamically adjusts the size of the training window and accordingly, the rate of the model reconstruction. The calculations of the window size in OLIN are based on the information theory and statistics. The experimental results of [Last (2002)] show that in non-stationary data streams, dynamic windowing generates more accurate models than the static (fixed size) windowing approach used by CVFDT.

In [Cohen *et. al* (2004)], we have presented a new real-time data mining algorithm, called Incremental On-Line Information Network (IOLIN), which is an extension to the regenerative OLIN algorithm of [Last (2002)]. As shown by the empirical evaluation of [Cohen *et. al* (2004)], the IOLIN algorithm achieves almost the same and sometimes even higher accuracy rates than OLIN and it is significantly cheaper since it does not require producing a new model for every new window of examples. As long as no major concept drift is detected, the Incremental OLIN algorithm is applied repeatedly to a sliding window in order to update the current model rather than replace it completely. IOLIN re-generates a completely new model only in case of a major concept drift, which is associated with a statistically significant rise in the classification error rate. The increased processing rate of IOLIN (measured in records per second) makes it a better tool for dealing with high rates of data arrival, like in case of dynamic web traffic data.

3.3.5   *Input-Output Analysis of Software Systems*

A recent study by the US National Institute of Standards & Technology [NIST (2002)] found that "the national annual costs of an inadequate infrastructure for software testing is estimated to range from 22.2 to 59.5 billion" (p. ES-3) or about 0.6 percent of the US gross domestic product. This number does not include costs associated with catastrophic failures of mission-critical software (such as the Patriot Missile Defense System failure in 1991 and the 165 million Mars Polar Lander shutdown in 1999). According to another report, U.S. Department of Defense alone loses over four billion dollars a year due to software failures. Recently, a programming error has been identified as the cause of alarm failures that might have contributed to the scope of 2003 summer's Northeast blackout [AP (2004)]. At the conceptual level, there is no difference between the effects of a software programming error, the effects of a user mistake or the effects of someone deliberately changing the system behavior. Consequently, the same procedures can be applied for discovering malicious and faulty code in a software system.

The ultimate goal of system-level functional testing is to verify that the system performs its functions as specified in the requirements and there are no hidden errors or "logic bombs" left. In the view of continual changes faced by any software system, the most important and extensive form of testing is regression testing, which is aimed at verifying that the system basic functionality has not changed as a result of adding new features, correcting existing faults or introducing malicious code. Since proving the code correctness is not feasible for large software systems, the practical testing is limited to a series of experiments showing the program behavior in certain situations. Each choice of input testing data is called a test case. Ideally, a minimal set of regression test cases can be generated from a complete and up-to-date specification of functional requirements. Unfortunately, frequent changes make the original requirements documentation, even if once complete and accurate, hardly relevant to the new versions of software [El-Ramly *et. al* (2002)]. Certain specified behaviors of the system may be implemented in a different way or completely omitted from the system. At the same time, some implemented behavior may not be specified at all, which is especially true for any kind of malicious code (viruses, worms,

Trojan horses, etc.).

To ensure effective design of test cases, one has to recover (reverse engineer) the actual requirements of an existing system. Recovery of missing requirements in computational and data-driven systems (having multiple inputs and outputs) can be based on an empirical observation that not all program inputs influence every output [Schroeder *et. al* (2000)]. Identification of a set of input variables that influence the computation of every output is called input-output analysis. In [Schroeder *et. al* (2000)], several ways are proposed to determine input-output relationships in tested software. These include analysis of system specifications, structural analysis of the system's source code, and observing the results of system execution. While, as indicated above, available system specifications may be incomplete or outdated, especially in the case of a "legacy" application, and the code may be poorly structured and documented, the data provided by the system execution seems to be the most reliable source of information on the actual functionality of a monitored system.

In [Last *et. al* (2004); Last *et. al* (2003); Last *et. al* (2004)], we have introduced the idea that input-output analysis of execution data can be automated by data mining classification algorithms such as the IFN (Info-Fuzzy Network) methodology [Last *et. al* (2004); Maimon *et. al* (2000)]. The general scheme of the IFN-based input-output analysis is shown in Figure 3.3. Random Tests Generator (RTG) obtains the list of system inputs and outputs along with their types (discrete, continuous, etc.) from the system interface. The data-mining algorithm (IFN) is trained on inputs provided by RTG and outputs obtained from a stable version of the system by means of the Test Bed module. In [Last *et. al* (2004)], a separate IFN model is built for each output variable. Alternatively, a single model can be induced for all system outputs using a multi-output data mining algorithm such as M-IFN [Last (2004)]. The following information can be derived from each IFN model: a set of input attributes relevant to each output, logical (if then) rules expressing the relationships between the selected input attributes and the corresponding output, equivalence classes in the range of each input, and a set of non-redundant test cases. The induced IFN model can also be used to predict the most probable value of the output in each test case and to evaluate the correctness of actual outputs produced by a new, possibly faulty version of the tested system. A highly unlikely output may be an indication of an unintentional programming error or a malicious modification of the original code. Thus, in [Last *et. al* (2004)], our method has successfully detected five errors randomly injected in the code of a complex software program for solving partial differential equations.

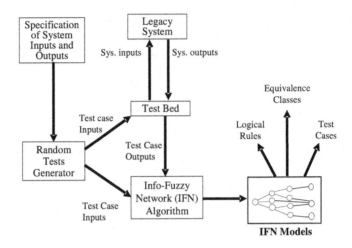

Fig. 3.3   IFN-Based IO Analysis: The Training Phase

3.4   Summary

In this chapter, we have demonstrated the wide potential of employing data mining techniques in the global campaign against terrorists using (actually, misusing) the cyber space in their criminal interests. As demonstrated by several other chapters of this volume, applications of data mining technology to information warfare are in no way limited to the methods covered in Section 3.3 above. We believe that as computers become more powerful and the web users become better connected to each other we will see more information technologies aiding in the war on terror on one side, along with a higher level of cyber terror sophistication on the other side. Leaving data mining out of this technological race is just not an option.

Bibliography

Associated Press, Software Bug Linked To Blackout, InformationWeek, Feb. 13, [http://informationweek.com/story/showArticle.jhtml?articleID=17700018]

Ben-Dov, M., Wu, W., Feldman, R. and Cairns, P.A. (2004). Improving Knowledge Discovery by Combining Text-Mining & Link Analysis Techniques, *Workshop on Link Analysis, Counter-terrorism, and Privacy, in conjunction with SIAM International Conference on Data Mining*, Lake Buena Vista, Florida, April 22–24.

Cesarano, C., d'Acierno, A., Picariello, A. (2003). An Intelligent Search Agent System for Semantic Information Retrieval on the Internet, *Proc. of the Fifth ACM International Workshop on Web Information and Data Management*, November 7-8, 2003, New Orleans, Louisiana, USA, pp. 111–117.

Chang, G., Healey, M.J., McHugh, J.A.M. and Wang, J.T.L. (2001). Mining the World Wide Web — An Information Search Approach, *Kluwer Academic Publishers*.

Cohen, L., Avrahami, G. and Last, M. (2004). Incremental Info-Fuzzy Algorithm for Real Time Data Mining of Non-Stationary Data Streams, *Proc. of TDM 2004 — ICDM 2004 Workshop on Temporal Data Mining: Algorithms, Theory and Applications*, November 01–04, Brighton, UK.

Corbin, J. (2002). Al-Qaeda: In Search of the Terror Network that Threatens the World, *Thunder's Mouth Press / Nation Books*, New York.

Corera, G. (2004). Web Wise Terror Network, *BBC NEWS: 2004/10/06*, [http://news.bbc.co.uk/go/pr/fr/-/1/hi/world/3716908.stm].

Cyber-terrorism, Foreign Report, London, 25 September, 1997.

Domingos, P. and Hulten, G. (2000). Mining High-Speed Data Streams, *Proc. of KDD 2000*, pp 71–80.

Domingos, P. and Hulten, G. (2001). Mining Time-Changing Data Streams, *Proc. of KDD 2001*, pp. 97–106, ACM Press.

El-Ramly, M., Stroulia, E. and Sorenson, P. (2002). From Run-time Behavior to Usage Scenarios: An Interaction-pattern Mining Approach, *Proc. of KDD-2002, Edmonton, Canada*, July, ACM Press, pp. 315–327.

Fayyad, U., Piatetsky-Shapiro, G. and Smyth, P. (1996). From Data Mining to Knowledge Discovery: An Overview. *U. Fayyad, G. Piatetsky-Shapiro, P.*

Smyth, and R. Uthurusamy (Eds.), Advances in Knowledge Discovery and Data Mining, pp. 1–30, AAAI/MIT Press.

Feldman, R., Regev, Y., Finkelstein-Landau, M., Hurvitz E. and Kogan, B. (2002). Mining Biomedical Literature Using Information Extraction, *Current Drug Discovery*, pp. 19–23, October.

Han, J. and Kamber, M. (2001). Data Mining: Concepts and Techniques, *Morgan Kaufmann*.

Hill, M. (2004). U.S. Funds Chat-Room Surveillance Study, *Associated Press*, October 11.

Holmes, C. (2004). Panel Discusses Threat of Cyberterrorism, *Workshop, The Cornell Daily Sun*, November 12, [http://www.cornellsun.com].

Jain, A.K., Murty, M.N. and Flynn, P.J. (1999). Data Clustering: A Review, *ACM Computing Surveys*, **31(3)**, September.

Jatowt A. and Ishizuka, M. (2004). Summarization of Dynamic Content in Web Collections, *J.-F. Boulicaut, F. Esposito, F. Giannotti, and D. Pedreschi (Eds.), Knowledge Discovery In Databases PKDD-2004: 8th European Conference on Principles and Practice of Knowledge Discovery in Databases*, Lecture Notes in Computer Science, Springer Verlag, pp. 245–254.

Kandel, A., Pacheco, R., Martins, A. and Khator, S. (1996). The Foundations of Rule-Based Computations in Fuzzy Models. *Fuzzy Modelling, Paradigms and Practice, W. Pedrycz (Eds.)*, Kluwer, Boston, pp. 231–263.

Khosla, P.K. (2004). Beating The Cyber Threat, *Chief Executive*, December, **204**, [http://www.chiefexecutive.net/mag/204/].

Klusch, M. (2001). Information Agent Technology for the Internet: A Survey, *Journal on Data and Knowledge Engineering, Special Issue on Intelligent Information Integration, D. Fensel (Ed.)*, **36(3)**, Elsevier Science.

Last, M. (2002). Online Classification of Nonstationary Data Streams, *Intelligent Data Analysis*, **6(2)**, pp. 129–147.

Last, M. (2004). Multi-Objective Classification with Info-Fuzzy Networks, *Proc. of the 15th European Conference on Machine Learning (ECML 2004)*, Pisa, Italy, Springer-Verlag, Lecture Notes in Artificial Intelligence 3201, pp. 239–249, September.

Last, M. and Friedman, M. (2004). Automated Detection of Injected Faults in a Differential Equation Solver, *Proc. of the Eighth IEEE International Symposium on High Assurance Systems Engineering (HASE04)*, Tampa, FL, USA, pp. 265–266, 25–26 March.

Last, M., Friedman, M. and Kandel, A. (2003). The Data Mining Approach to Automated Software Testing, *Proc. of the Ninth ACM SIGKDD International Conference on Knowledge Discovery and Data Mining (KDD-2003)*, pp. 388–396, Washington, DC, USA August 24–27.

Last, M., Friedman, M. and Kandel, A. (2004). Using Data Mining for Automated Software Testing, *International Journal of Software Engineering and Knowledge Engineering (IJSEKE), Special Issue on Data Mining for Software Engineering and Knowledge Engineering*, **14(4)**, pp. 369–393, August.

Last, M. and Kandel, A. (1999). Automated Perceptions in Data Mining, invited paper, *Proc. IEEE International Fuzzy Systems Conference, 1999*, Part I, pp. 190–197, Seoul, Korea, August.

Last, M. and Kandel, A. (2002). Perception-based Analysis of Engineering Experiments in Semiconductor Industry, *International Journal of Image and Graphics*, **2(1)**, pp. 107–126.

Last, M. and Maimon, O. (2004). A Compact and Accurate Model for Classification, *IEEE Transactions on Knowledge and Data Engineering*, **16(2)**, pp. 203–215, February.

Lent, B., Agrawal, R. and Srikant, R. (1997). Discovering Trends in Text Databases, *Proc. of the 3rd International Conference on Knowledge Discovery and Data Mining*, pp. 227–230, California.

Lipton E. and Lichtblau, E. (2004). Even Near Home, a New Front Is Opening in the Terror Battle, *The New York Times*, September 23.

Maimon, O. and Last, M. (2000). Knowledge Discovery and Data Mining - The Info-Fuzzy Network (IFN) Methodology, *Kluwer Academic Publishers, Massive Computing*, Boston, December.

Mena, J. (1999). Homeland Security Techniques and Technologies, *Charles River Media*.

Menczer, F., Monge, A.E. (19990. Scalable Web Search by Adaptive Online Agents: An InfoSpiders Case Study, *M. Klusch (Ed.), Intelligent Information Agents, Springer*.

Mendez-Torreblanca, A., Montes-y-Gomez, M. and Lopez-Lopez, A. (2002). A Trend Discovery System for Dynamic Web Content Mining, *Proc. of CIC-2002*.

Mitchell, T.M. (1997). Machine Learning, *McGraw-Hill*.

Mladenic, D. (1999). Text-Learning and Related Intelligent Agents: A Survey, *IEEE Intelligent Systems*, pp. 44–54, July/August.

Mladenic, D. (1996). Personal WebWatcher: Design and Implementation. *Technical Report IJS-DP-7472, School of Computer Science, Carnegie-Mellon University*, Pittsburgh, USA, October.

National Institute of Standards & Technology. The Economic Impacts of Inadequate Infrastructure for Software Testing. *Planning Report 02-3*, May, 2002.

Pant, G., Srinivasan, P. and Menczer, F. (2004). Crawling the Web, *M. Levene and A. Poulovassilis (Eds.), Web Dynamics, Springer*.

Popp, R., Armour, T., Senator, T. and Numrich, K. (2004). Countering Terrorism through Information Technology, *Communications of the ACM*, **47(3)**, March.

Provost, F. and Fawcett, T. (2001). Robust Classification for Imprecise Environments, *Machine Learning*, **42(3)**, pp. 203–231.

Quinlan, J.R. (1993). C4.5: Programs for Machine Learning, *Morgan Kaufmann*.

Schroeder, P.J. and Korel, B. (2000). Black-Box Test Reduction Using Input-Output Analysis. *In Proc. of ISSTA '00*, pp. 173–177.

Srikant R. and Agrawal, R. (1996). Mining Quantitative Association Rules in Large Relational Tables. *Proc. of ACM-SIGMOD 1996 Conference on Management of Data*.

Sullivan, D. (Ed.) and Sherman, C. (Associate Editor) (2004). Search Engine

Watch, [www.searchenginewatch.com].

The 9/11 Commission Report: Final Report of the National Commission on Terrorist Attacks on the Unites States, *New York: W.W. Norton & Co.,* 2004.

Walla, March 13, 2004, [www.walla.co.il].

Widmer, G. and Kubat, M. (1996). Learning in the Presence of Concept Drift and Hidden Contexts, *Machine Learning,* **23(1)**, pp. 69–101.

Yu, E.S., Koo, P.C. and Liddy, E.D. (2000). Evolving intelligent text-based agents, *Proc. of the Fourth International Conference on Autonomous agents,* Barcelona, Spain, pp. 388–395.

Zeller, T. 92004). On the Open Internet, a Web of Dark Alleys, *The New York Times,* December 20.

Chapter 4

A Content-Based Model for Web-Monitoring

Bracha Shapira

Department of Information Systems Engineering,
Ben-Gurion University of the Negev, Beer-Sheva 84105, Israel
E-mail: bshapira@bgumail.bgu.ac.il

Anomaly Detection Systems (ADS) aim at detecting abnormal users based on their irregular behavior in a certain environment. The model presented here is related to anomaly detection having the same goals of detecting irregular users. However, ADS monitor users' actions while we look at the **content** of users' actions and attempt to detect irregular users by the irregular content that they are looking at. The model has two possible modes. One is the "similarity" mode on which the detection is based on similarity of the content of suspicious users' to known "irregular" content. The other is the "dissimilarity" mode on which detection is based on dissimilarity between the content suspicious users access and known "regular" content in a certain environment. The model has two phases, a learning phase on which the system is trained with regular or irregular content (according to the mode), and a detection phase on which the model compares monitored data to trained data in order to detect suspicious users.

4.1 Introduction

This chapter describes a unique content-based anomaly detection model to detect abnormal activities on the Web. Anomaly detection relies on models of the intended behavior of users and applications and interprets deviations from this "normal" behavior as evidence of malicious activity ([Tan and Maxion (2002)], [Ghosh *et. al* (1998)] and [Lane and Brodley (1998)]).

The underlying intuitive assumption of this model is that content of users browsing reflects their interests. This assumption is the basis of the many personalization models, algorithms and systems ([Mobasher *et. al* (2002)]) that generate user "profiles" from the content of pages they browse. A stronger assumption is that users that have similar interests could be identified by the content of their browse and represented as a group of users or stereotypes. Individual user profiles can then be compared to those stereotypes to identify whether they relate to any of these groups. This assumption is the basis for numerous collaboration filtering systems ([Hanani *et. al* (20002)]) on which users are offered documents or knowledge that was judged as relevant by members of the stereotypes that the users relate to. For example in Amazon – customers are offered products that were judged relevant by similar customers (or customers of the same "stereotype"). These two assumptions were used by the model presented here to detect users with desired properties on the Web by the content of the pages they browse. The model may have a wide range of applications all referring to the detection of groups of users that have common interests. Example of such applications include security related application such as terrorist or pedophile detection as well as commercial-related application such as targeting products to customers with certain common characteristics.

We suggest a new type of behavior-based anomaly detection model that uses the content of web pages browsed by a specific group of users as an input for detecting abnormal activity. In this study, we refer to the *textual* content of web pages only, excluding images, music, video clips, and other complex data types. The model has two modes of activation that can also be integrated.

The first is the "similar" mode that looks for users similar to a known group of abnormal users. Users who are similar (above a defined threshold of similarity) to the abnormal group are considered as related to that group. For example, the system might maintain information about pedophiles, and look for suspected users, i.e., users with similar interests to the pedophiles group.

The second mode is the "dissimilar mode" that maintains information about the interests of "normal" users in a certain environment (such as a campus or organization), and detects users that are dissimilar (under a defined threshold of similarity) to the normal group.

These two modes could be integrated to a combined model that first detects abnormal users and then tries to relate them to one or more known abnormal groups. For example, a system might look for abnormal students in a university campus, once such a student is detected, it can be compared to known abnormal users such as pedophiles or terrorists. We assume that content normally viewed by the group's users represent their information needs and can be used as input data for learning the group's users normal behavior and for detecting an abnormal user. We define user abnormal behavior as an access to information that is not expected to be viewed by a normal member of the group.

The general architecture of the proposed system is described in Fig. 4.1. Each user is identified by a "user's computer" having a unique IP address rather than by his or her name. This is done in order to preserve users' privacy. The *Detector* collects the data passing through the net to and from public data repositories (i.e., the Internet) on real-time and compares the data from each user to the database of known groups. Depending on the mode (similar or dissimilar), the detector issues an alarm upon high similarity of a user to known groups while activated in the similar more, or upon high dissimilarity between a user and the "normal" users when activated in the dissimilar mode. In case of a real-time alarm, the detected IP can be used to locate the computer and hopefully the abnormal user himself who may still be logged on to the same computer. The next section details the model.

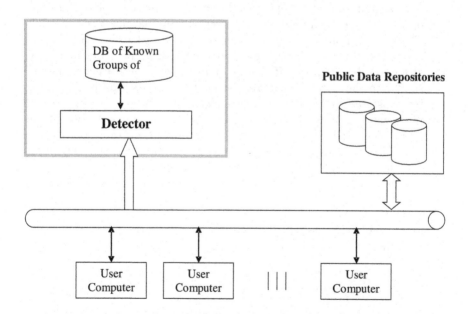

Fig. 4.1 Suggested IDS Architecture and Environment

4.2   Detailed Description of the Model

The suggested model has two phases, a learning phase and a detection phase:

(1) The learning phase — during learning, the web traffic of a group of users (content of publicly available web pages) is recorded and transformed to an efficient representation for further analysis. We use the vector representation, i.e. each page is transformed to a vector of weighted terms. When activated in the similar mode, the learning phase is applied on pages related to the group of users to be learned, for example, if the system detects terrorist, the learning phase would be applied on collected terror-related pages that represent terrorist interests. When activated in the dissimilar mode, the learning phase is applied on the same environment where the detection would later be applied in order to learn the "normal" content of users in the environment. The collected data is used to derive and represent the group's areas of interest by applying a statistical technique called cluster-analysis that groups similar items into a unique representation. The learning phase is a preprocessing task and is performed in batch to create the DB of groups of users that is then used in the detection phase on-line.

(2) The detection phase – The detection mode is aimed at detecting abnormal users. If the similar mode is activated, users similar to the defined group are detected, and if the dissimilar mode is activated, users dissimilar to the normal users are detected. The detection is performed by transforming the content of each page accessed by a user to a vector representation that can be compared against the representation of the groups for similarity or dissimilarity (depending on the mode). The number of suspicious accesses, and the period of time required in order to issue an alarm about a user are defined by the detection algorithm. The detection is performed on-line and should therefore be efficient and scalable.

In the following sub-sections, we describe in details the learning and the detection phases.

4.2.1   *Learning Phase*

The learning phase of the model results with a DB including representations of the interests of the users group. During the detection phase users accessed pages are compared to this Data-Base. Fig. 4.2 is a graphical description of the learning phase.

The difference between the learning phase activated in the similar mode and the learning phase activated in the dissimilar mode is that for the similar mode ,the system is provided with a set of pages, manually collected by experts that know the group to be detected. For example, to generate groups of terror-related interests, terror-experts provide the model with sites of terror related content for the training of the system.

For a learning phase of the dissimilar mode that system has to listen to "normal" users in the monitored environment for a period of time and collect pages to represent the "normal" users groups.

The learning phase consists of the *Filter, Vectors-Generator* and the *Clusters-Generator* components. Following is a description of the functionality of these components:

Each page of the training data is sent to the *Filter* for exclusion of non-appropriate pages, i.e. pages that do not include enough meaningful textual information. The *Filter* also removes images tags related to the content format (for example, the tags of an HTML document are filtered out) from the appropriate pages. The filtered pages are sent to the *Vectors-Generator* component that transforms each page to a weighted terms vector. The vector entries represent terms and their values represent the weight of the terms so that weights>0 correspond to terms that are meaningful and may represent the page. The higher the weight, the higher is the importance of the term to the page. The weight is defined by the relative frequency of the term to the page, and by other factors such as the position of the term in the page (e.g., terms appearing in the title receive high weight). The vectors are recorded for the clustering process that follows.

The *Clusters-Generator* module (Fig. 4.2) receives the vectors generated by the *Vectors-Generator* and performs cluster-analysis on these vectors. Cluster-analysis is a process that receives as input a set of objects with attributes and generates clusters (groups) of similar objects, so that the objects within a group have high similarity (measured for the attributes) and the objects between groups are dissimilar. The objects in this model are the pages, where the attributes are the terms. The clustering process would group similar pages in a cluster, meaning that pages related to similar topics are grouped in one cluster. The n clusters generated by the *Cluster-Generator* represent the n areas of interest of the defined group of users. The optimal n is defined by the clustering algorithm. For each cluster, the *Group-Representor* component computes a central vector (centroid) – denoted by Cv_i for clustrer I - which is an average vector over the vectors of the cluster which represents the cluster. In our model each centroid represents one area of interest of the group of users (the special group in the similar mode and the "normal" users in the dissimilar mode). The output of the learning phase is a set of vectors (the centroids of the clusters) corresponding to the areas of interest of the group. The learning phase is a batch process and should be activated regularly once in a period of time to maintain up to date representation of the group.

4.2.2   *The Detection Phase*

During the detection phase, a group of computers in a certain environment is monitored to detect abnormal users. The content of transactions of the group members is collected on-line (see Fig. 4.3) and compared to the set of pre-defined centroids (that were generated during the learning phase). The detection phase consists of the *Sniffer*, *Filter*, the *Vector–Generator* and the *Detector* which is the main component of this phase. The *Sniffer* captures the pages that users (identified) by their Ips, access at the network layer and sends each page to the *Filter* for further processing. The *Filter* and the *Vector-Generator* have the same functionality as in the learning phase, i.e., each page is transformed into a vector of weighted terms. The Detector receives the vectors (and their Ips) and decides whether a vector is too similar or too dissimilar – depending on the activation mode to the DB of user groups. The *Detector* measures the distance between each vector and each of the centroids representing an area of interest to the user. The detection algorithms can be calibrated with certain parameters to fine-tune the detection.

Some of the parameters are:

(1) The similarity or dissimilarity threshold – depending on the activation mode.
(2) The number of accesses by the same IP that would issue an alarm.
(3) The time frame of suspicious accesses that by the same IP that would issue an alarm.

The detection algorithm issues an alarm in when all conditions of the parameters are satisfied. The alarm consists of the suspicious along with the data that causes the issuing of an alarm. The similarity between the vectors accessed by users and the centroids might be measured using any known distance measuring methods between vectors, such as the Euclidean distance, or inner products. We apply the Cosine measure that captures the similarity between the directions of the vectors so that absolute weightings won't affect the similarity but the relation between the term weights (correlation). The detector issues the alarm when the similarity between the access vector and the nearest centroid is lower than the threshold denoted by tr or when the distance is above tr (depending) on the activation mode.

The following is the Cosine equation used:

$$Min \left(\frac{\sum\limits_{i=1}^{m} (tCv_{i1} \cdot tAv_i)}{\sqrt{\sum\limits_{i=1}^{m} tCv_{i1}^2 \cdot \sum\limits_{i=1}^{m} tAv_i^2}}, ..., \frac{\sum\limits_{i=1}^{m} (tCv_{in} \cdot tAv_i)}{\sqrt{\sum\limits_{i=1}^{m} tCv_{in}^2 \cdot \sum\limits_{i=1}^{m} tAv_i^2}} \right) < tr$$

where Cv_i is the ith centroid vector, Av - the access vector, tCv_{i1} - the ith term in the vector Cv_i, tAv_i- the ith term in the vector Av, and m – the number of unique terms in each vector.

4.3   Summary

This chapter presents a unique content-based anomaly detection model to detect abnormal users on the Web. This model might be applied to detect any group of users that have common interests and thus browse sites with similar contents. The model first "learns" the group of users at batch and then monitors users as they browse on-line and issues an alarm once a suspicious user is detected. A system that implements the model has to consider efficiency issues to enable monitoring of many users while they browse and issue an alarm at real time so that the user might be located at the IP while still browsing. Feasibility of such system depends on fast and effective implementation of the representation of the Web pages, so that the representation would be derived on real-time and would be memory efficient, but still represent the page accurate enough, i.e., the main topics of the page are captured and can be accurately compared to the known topics in the system. The next chapter describes a system that is based on the model and proves its feasibility. The model applied a simple vector-based representation of Web-pages that is known to work pretty well in many Information Retrieval applications ([Salton and Buckley (1998)]).. However, the vector space model assumes term independency so that the context of terms is not identified. A more sophisticated context-based representation of Web-based might be applied to the model possible better result.

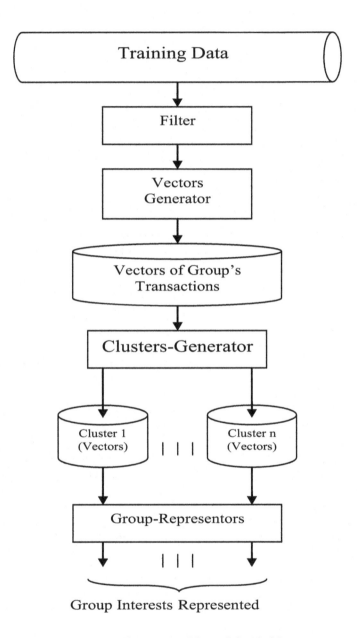

Fig. 4.2 The Learning Phase of the Model

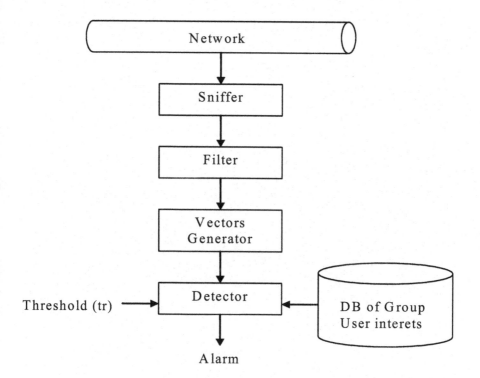

Fig. 4.3   The Detection Phase

Bibliography

Ghosh, A.K., Wanken, J. and Charron, F. (1998). Detecting Anomalous and Unknown Intrusions Against Programs, *Proc. Annual Computer Security Applications Conference*, ACSAC'98, pp. 259–267.

Hanani, U., Shapira, B. and Shoval, P. (2002). Information Filtering: Overview of Issues, Research and Systems, User Modeling and User-Adapted Interaction 11, pp. 203–259.

Lane, T. and Brodley, C.E. (1998). Temporal sequence learning and data reduction for anomaly detection, *Proc. 5th ACM conference on Computer and communications security*, pp. 150–158.

Mobasher, B., Cooley, R. and Srivastava, J. (2002). Automatic personalization based on Web usage mining, *J. Communications of the ACM* **43**, 8, pp. 142–151.

Salton, G. and Buckley, C. (1998). Term-Weighting Approaches in Automatic Text Retrieval, *J. Information Processing and Management* **24**, 5, pp. 513–523.

Tan, K. and Maxion, R. (2002). Why 6? Defining the Operational Limits of Stide, an Anomaly-Based Intrusion Detector. *Proc. IEEE Symposium on Security and Privacy*, pp. 188–202.

Chapter 5

TDS — An Innovative Terrorist Detection System

Yuval Elovici

Department of Information Systems Engineering,
Ben-Gurion University of the Negev, Beer-Sheva 84105, Israel
E-mail: elovici@bgumail.bgu.ac.il

The Terrorist Detection System (TDS) is aimed at tracking down suspected terrorists by analyzing the content of information they access. TDS operates in two modes: a training mode and a detection mode. During the training mode TDS is provided with Web pages accessed by a normal group of users and computes their typical interests. During the detection mode TDS performs real-time monitoring of the traffic emanating from the monitored group of users, analyzes the content of the Web pages accessed, and generates an alarm if the users access information is not within the typical interests of the group. TDS was implemented and evaluated in a network environment of 38 users where three users imitated suspected terrorists by accessing to terror related sites. TDS detection performance was compared to the performance of the Intrusion Detection System (IDS) based on anomaly detection and was found to be superior.

5.1 Introduction

Due to the availability and publishing ease of information on the Web, terrorists increasingly exploit the Internet as a communication, intelligence, and propaganda tool where they can safely communicate with their affiliates, coordinate action plans, raise funds, and introduce new supporters into their networks ([Birnhack and Elkin-Koren (2002)], [Lemos (2002)] and [Kelley (2002)]). Governments and intelligence agencies are trying to identify terrorist activities on the Web in order to prevent future acts of terror

75

([Ingram (2001)]). Thus, there is a need for new methods and technologies to assist in this cyber intelligence effort.

By means of content monitoring and analysis of Web pages accessed by a group of Web surfers, it is possible to infer surfers areas of interest ([Elovici *et. al* (2003)]). Using this approach, a real time Web traffic monitoring could be performed to identify terrorists as they access their information of interest on the Internet ([Elovici *et. al* (2003)], [Last *et. al* (2003a)]).

In this chapter a new system named Terrorist Detection System (TDS) is presented aimed at tracking down suspected terrorists by analyzing the content of information that they access. The system operates in two modes: a training mode that may be activated off-line, and a detection mode that operates in real-time. In the training mode TDS is provided with Web pages of normal users from which, it derive their normal behavior profile by applying data mining algorithms to the training data. In the detection mode TDS performs real-time monitoring of the traffic emanating from the monitored group of users, analyzes the content of the Web pages they access, and generates an alarm if a user accesses to information that is not expected from a normal user.

The reminder of the chapter is organized as follows. In the second section a brief review on Content-Based Methodology for Anomaly Detection on the Web is presented. TDS is based on this methodology. In the third section the design goals behind the development of TDS are portrayed. In the fourth section TDS architecture is described in detail. The performance measures used to evaluate TDS are discussed in the fifth section. In the sixth section, the evaluation of TDS is illustrated. The section 5.7 elaborates on the ways TDS can be deployed. Finally, the eighth section outlines directions for the next stages of TDS development.

5.2 Content-Based Methodology for Anomaly Detection: Review

TDS is based on the Content-Based Methodology for Anomaly Detection on the Web that was suggested by Last ([Last *et. al* (2003b)]). The methodology contains two parts. In the first, normal users profile is derived based on the content of information they access, and in the second abnormal users are detected by monitoring the content of information they access and comparing it with the normal users profile. This section will present a review on this methodology. Subsection 5.2.1 presents normal user profile (hereafter named normal user behavior) computation and subsection 5.2.2 presents the abnormal user detection.

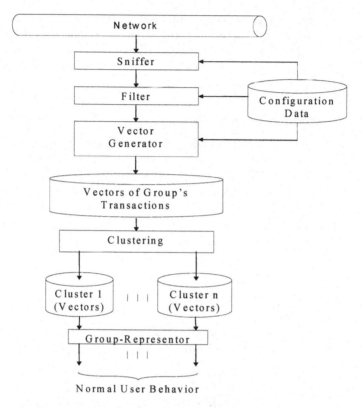

Fig. 5.1   Learning the normal user behavior

5.2.1   *Learning the Normal User Behavior*

In the first part of the Content-Based Methodology for Anomaly Detection, the normal user behavior is derived by monitoring and processing the content of information that normal users are accessing (see Fig. 5.1). The sniffer module intercepts packets of users that are under surveillance and sends them to the filter module. The filter module filters out packets that do not include HTML textual content, and reconstructs them into original HTML pages. The reconstructed HTML pages are sent to the vector generator module that converts each page into a vector of weighted terms.

During the learning phase all the vectors are stored in vectors of group transactions DB. When there are enough vectors in the DB, a clustering algorithm is applied on the vectors. The clustering process generates several clusters, each cluster including vectors relating to the different information interests of the normal users. A centroid vector is computed for each cluster and these centroids represents the information interests of normal users (normal user behavior). The normal user behavior will be used during the detection part of the methodology to detect abnormal users.

5.2.2 *Detecting Abnormal Users*

In the second part of the Content-Based Methodology for Anomaly Detection, the users are being monitored and abnormal users are detected (see Fig. 5.2). The sniffer, filtering, and vector generator modules are the same as in the first part of the methodology. Each vector that represents an HTML page that was intercepted is compared with normal user behavior by the detecting module. The threshold tr controls the sensitivity of the detection process.

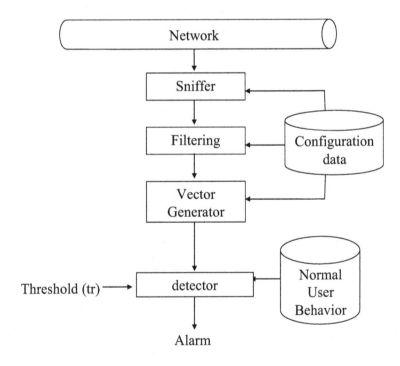

Fig. 5.2   Detecting abnormal users

5.3 Design Goals

The design goals behind the development of TDS are:

(1) Detecting terrorist activities based on the Content-Based Methodology for Anomaly Detection — TDS should be able to detect terrorist related activities by monitoring the network traffic content. TDS should focus only on network traffic content containing textual HTML pages. In order to achieve this goal TDS has to be able to disregard irrelevant network traffic content.

(2) On-line detection — TDS should be able to detect on-line a suspected terrorist that is accessing terrorist related content. Such on-line detection may enable law enforcement agencies to arrest suspected terrorists accessing the Web through public infrastructure such as a public computer lab in a university campus or Internet cafe. The detection result will include the suspected terrorist IP. The connection between IP and the real user identity is beyond the scope of this design.

(3) Detection should be based on passive eavesdropping on the network — TDS should monitor the network traffic without being noticed by the suspected users or the monitored infrastructure provider. Passive eavesdropping can be achieved by a network snifter or by installing an agent in computers acting as proxy.

(4) Page loss should be less than 5% — TDS should be designed such that while monitoring the traffic content it will be able to detect 95% of the monitored traffic pages. This design goal is important in order to get a reasonable detection rate.

(5) Being able to cope with packet loss — Every network sniffer suffers from packet loss and TDS is based on such sniffers. TDS should be able to cope with packet loss (being able to reconstruct parts of the HTML page even when some of the packets are missing).

5.4 TDS Architecture

TDS architecture is based on the Content-Based Methodology for Anomaly Detection described in section 5.2. It includes four components:

- **Online-HTML Tracer (OHT)** – is responsible for intercepting network packets, filtering out packets that do not contain HTML pages, and reconstructing the textual content of the HTML pages. Subsection 5.4.1 will elaborate on this component.
- **Vectorization** – is responsible for converting the textual content of an HTML page into a vector of weighted terms. The vectorization module

is further explained is subsection 5.4.2.

- **Normal User Behavior Computation** – is responsible for computing the normal user behavior based on pages being accessed by normal
  users. This module is further explained in subsection 5.4.3.
- **Detection** – is responsible for comparing a vector of an intercepted
  page with the normal user behavior, and raise an alarm. The detection
  module algorithm is described in subsection 5.4.4.

The TDS architecture is described in Fig. 5.3.

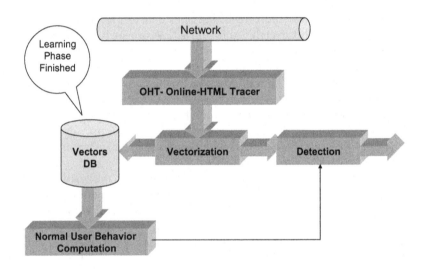

Fig. 5.3   TDS Architecture

TDS operates in two modes: learning and detecting. During the learning
mode the OHT component intercepts HTML pages, converts them into
vectors, and store them in the vectors DB implemented as a directory where
each vector is stored in a separate file. When there are enough vectors
(user defined parameter) the normal user behavior computation component
computes the normal user behavior. The computed normal user behavior
is sent to the detection module.

During the detection mode, the OHT component intercepts HTML
pages. The pages are converted to vectors and sent to the detector component. The detector component compare the vectors with the normal user
behavior and based on this comparison raises an alarm.

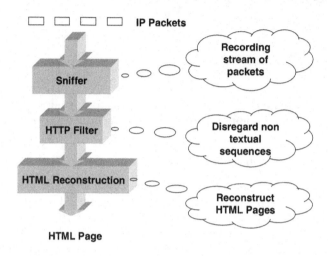

Fig. 5.4   On-Line HTML Tracer

5.4.1   *On-line HTML Tracer*

The On-Line HTML Tracer component described in Fig. 5.4 implements
the sniffer and the filtering modules (see Fig. 5.1) of the Content-Based
Methodology for Anomaly Detection. Its first module is a sniffer implemented by using the WinPickup (http://winpcap.polito.it) software tool.
The packets intercepted by the sniffer module are sent to the HTTP filter
module. This module inspects the content of each intercepted packet and
filters out packets that do not contain textual HTML pages. Packets that
contain textual HTML are reconstructed into HTML pages by the HTML
reconstruction module. The reconstructed HTML pages are sent to the
vectorization component.

5.4.2   *Vectorization*

The vectorization component is implemented by the Extractor ([extractor
(2003)]) software tool. This tool receives an HTML page and generates a

1. Terrorist	3.5
2. Bomb	3.2
3. Computer	
.	
.	
.	
30. Send	0.1

Fig. 5.5   Vectorization component

vector of weighted terms (see Fig. 5.5). Each vector includes up to 30 terms and for each term, its importance in the document is expressed by a score.

5.4.3   *Normal User Behavior Computation*

The normal user behavior computation component is based on the Vcluster program from the Cluto (www-users.cs.umn.edu/~karypis/cluto/download.html) Clustering Tool ([Karypis (2002)]). Vcluster is used to implement the clustering module (see Fig. 5.1) where the clustering algorithm used is 'k-way' and the similarity between the objects is computed using the cosine measure ([Boger *et. al* (2001)], [Pierrea *et. al* (2000)]). The 'k-way' clustering algorithm is a variation of the popular K-Means clustering algorithm.

This component operation is controlled by a parameter indicating the number of clusters to be generated. After activating the component, it clusters all the vectors in the DB and for each cluster a centroid vector is created. The output of this component is a set of centroids one for each cluster. This set is if fact the "normal user behavior" and it is used by the detector component.

5.4.4   *Detection*

The detection component (see Figure 5.6) receives vectors representing HTML pages accessed by users who are under surveillance. The vectors are stored in queues based on the user IP address such that each queue stores the last pages being accessed by a user. The size of the queue n is a system parameter. Upon updating the content of the queue, the detection component compares each vector in the queue with all the centroid vectors representing the normal user behavior. If k out of the n vectors in the queue $(k < n)$ are not similar to any of the vectors in the normal user behavior then the detection component raises an alarm. The similarity between the vectors (vectors and centroid vectors) is computed using the cosine measure ([Boger *et. al* (2001)], [Pierrea *et. al* (2000)]).

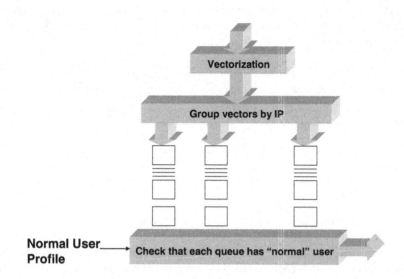

Fig. 5.6 Detection component

5.5 Performance Measures

To evaluate TDS performance the following measures (based on [Sequeira and Zaki (2002)]) were used:

Page loss rate (PLR): the percentage of textual HTML pages that the system did not manage to intercept and reconstruct out of the total number of pages transmitted on the communication line under surveillance by the system.

True Positive Rate (TP) (also known as Detection Rate or Completeness): the percentage of terrorist pages (abnormal) that the system managed to detect. In the experiments, terrorist pages will be obtained from the users simulating terrorists.

False Positive Rate (FP): the percentage of pages being accessed by normal users that the system incorrectly determined as related to terrorist activities.

Accuracy: percentage of alarms related to terrorist behavior out of the total number of alarms.

5.6   System Evaluation

TDS was evaluated on a small network of 38 computers having constant IP addresses. All computers accessed the Web through the same switch. The switch was programmed to send all the packets to one port where TDS server was connected.

Table 5.1   OHT Performance Evaluation

Maximal Time Gap	Captured HTML pages	Success Rate
25-60	3800	100%
20	3800	100%
15	3800	100%
10	3798	99.9%
5	3800	100%
0	3796	99.8%

In order to evaluate the page loss rate, 38 computers were configured to access a given list of 100 URLs that include textual HTML. The experiment included 13 iterations. If ideally performed, each iteration would result in 3800 reconstructed HTML pages. For every iteration, the time gap between accesses to the Web was controlled in order to test the frequency of accesses that the system is able to handle. The maximal time gap was set for each iteration; however, the exact time gap of accesses within iteration varied randomly in a range between zero and the maximal time gap. The first iteration was set to a maximal time gap of 60 seconds and the time gaps were decreased by five seconds on the following iterations. The evaluation results are shown in Table 5.1. OHT component managed to capture almost all the HTML pages being accessed from the 38 stations with a very high rate of success.

In order to evaluate the other performance measures of TDS, about 170,000 Web transactions (page views) were recorded over 24 days in order to learn the user normal behavior. Three users out of the 38 simulated suspicious behavior by accessing terror related Web sites. The TP and FP and the accuracy measures were evaluated when the system intercepted 200 pages, 100 pages of normal users and 100 pages of users simulating terrorist behavior. Each point in TP and FP ROC curves in Figs. 5.8 and 5.7 was computed for a different sensitivity level of the detection algorithm.

The results in Figs. 5.8 and 5.7 clearly suggest that the proposed methodology is feasible and a system implementing this methodology might reliably detect terrorists accessing the Internet based on the content of monitored Web traffic. In the experiments, TDS reached on average, TP=78% and FP=11.7% compared to TP=70% and FP=15% achieved by the AD-

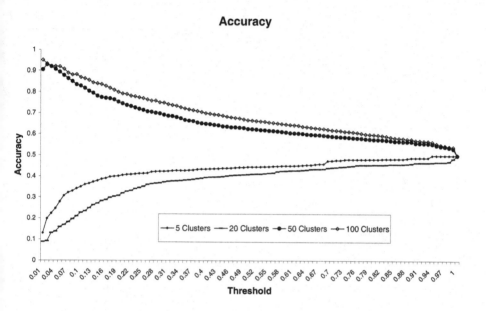

Fig. 5.7   TDS accuracy results

MIT system ([Sequeira and Zaki (2002)]), which utilized user command-level data.

5.7   System Deployment

TDS can be deployed in two different ways where each way has its advantages and disadvantages.

ISP-based: The system implementing the new methodology may be deployed within the ISP infrastructure. The major advantage of such a deployment is that the ISP is able to provide the exact identity of a suspicious user detected by the system since the IP is allocated to the user by the ISP. The disadvantages of such a deployment are that it requires ISP awareness and cooperation, and the privacy of the ISP subscribers is violated.

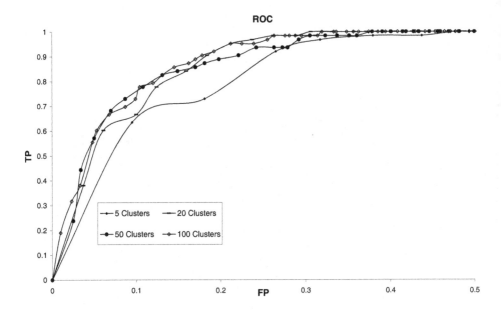

Fig. 5.8   TDS TP and FP results

Network-based System: The system implementing the new methodology is eavesdropping on communication lines connecting the ISPs to the Internet backbone. In such a deployment the major advantage is that ISP cooperation is not required and the privacy of the ISP subscribers is protected, since most ISPs are allocating a temporary IP address for every user. The major disadvantage of such a deployment is that the exact identity of a subscriber using a given IP address is unknown on-line.

It is difficult to effectively deploy a system based on the new methodology on sites providing internet access to casual users such as an Internet Cafe or Hot Spots since users are not required to identify themselves to the service operator.

5.8 Summary

The Terrorist Detection System (TDS) is aimed at tracking down suspected terrorists by analyzing the content of information that they access. TDS is based on the Content-Based Methodology for Anomaly Detection on the Web suggested by Last ([Last *et. al* (2003a)]). It operates in two modes: a training mode and a detection mode. During the training mode it computes the "normal user behavior" and during the detection mode TDS performs real-time monitoring of the traffic and generates an alarm if the user access information is not within the typical interests of the group (not similar to the computed normal user behavior).

The TDS system was implemented and evaluated in a network environment of 38 users where several users imitated suspected terrorists by accessing to terror related sites. TDS detection performance was compared with the performance of Intrusion Detection System (IDS) based on anomaly detection and was found to be superior.

An important contribution of TDS lies in the unique environment of its application. The detection component is planned to run in a real-time wide-area network environment and should be capable of on-line monitoring of many users. Therefore, a crucial design requirement was high-performance which called for enhancement of the algorithms involved especially the mining algorithm to high-performance and scalability.

TDS is an example of a successful application of data mining and machine learning techniques to the international cyber-war effort against world-wide terror.

Bibliography

Birnhack,N. and Elkin-Koren, N. (2002). Fighting Terror On-Line: The Legal Ramifications of September 11, The Law and Technology Center, Internal Report, Haifa University.
[http://law.haifa.ac.il/faculty/lec_papers/terror_info.pdf]

Boger, Z., Kuflik, T., Shoval, P. and Shapira, B. (2001). Automatic keyword identification by artificial neural networks compared to manual identification by users of filtering systems, *J. Information Processing and Management*, **37**, pp. 187–198.

Elovici, Y., Shapira, B., Last, M., Kandell, A. and Zaafrany, O. (2003). Using Data Mining Techniques for Detecting Terror-Related Activities on the Web, *J. of Information Warfare* **3(1)**, pp. 17–28.

Extractor DBI technologies (2003) [http://www.dbi-tech.com]

Fielding, R., Gettys, J. and Mogul, J. (1999). RFC2616: Hypertext Transfer Protocol — HTTP/1.1, Network Working Group.

Ingram, M. (2001). Internet privacy threatened following terrorist attacks on US, [http://www.wsws.org/articles/2001/sep2001/isps24.shtml]

Karypis, G. (2002). CLUTO — A Clustering Toolkit, Release 2.0, University of Minnesota,
[http://www.users.cs.umn.edu/~karypis/cluto/download.html]

Kelley, J. (2002). Terror Groups behind Web encryption, USA Today, [http://www.apfn.org/apfn/WTC_why.htm]

Last, M., Elovici, Y., Shapira, B., Zaafrany, O. and Kandel, A. (2003). Using Data Mining for Detecting Terror-Related Activities on the Web, *Proc. European Conference on Information Warfare and Security*, ECIW, pp 271–280.

Last, M., Elovici, Y., Shapira, B., Zaafrany, O. and Kandel, A. (2003). Content-Based Methodology for Anomaly Detection on the Web, Advances in Web Intelligence, E. Menasalvas et al. (Editors), *J. Springer-Verlag, Lecture Notes in Artificial Intelligence*, **2663**, pp. 113–123.

Lemos, R. (2002). What are the real risks of cyberterrorism?, ZDNet, [http://zdnet.com/2100-1105-955293.html]

Pierrea, S., Kacanb, C. and Probstc, W. (2000). An agent-based approach for integrating user profile into a knowledge management process, *J. Knowledge-Based Systems*, **13**, pp. 307–314.

Sequeira, K. and Zaki, M. (2002). ADMIT: Anomaly-based Data Mining for Intrusions, *Proc. SIGKDD'02*, pp. 386–395.

Winpcap version 3.0 (2004), http://winpcap.polito.it/

Wooster, R., Williams, S. and Brooks, P. (1996). HTTPDUMP: a network HTTP packet snooper.

Chapter 6

Clustering Algorithms for Variable-Length Vectors and Their Application to Detecting Terrorist Activities

Menahem Friedman

Department of Physics, Nuclear Research Center — Negev, Beer-Sheva, POB 9001, Israel and Department of Information Systems Engineering, Ben-Gurion University of the Negev, Beer-Sheva 84105, Israel E-mail: mlfrid@netvision.net.il

Moti Schneider

School of Computer Science, Netanya Academic College, Netanya, Israel Email: motis@netanya.ac.il

Abraham Kandel

Department of Computer Science and Engineering, University of South Florida, Tampa, FL 33620, USA and Faculty of Engineering, Tel-Aviv University, Tel-Aviv 69978, Israel Email: kandel@csee.usf.edu

6.1 Introduction

The war against terror, which is quickly becoming the greatest menace to the free world, has recently spread to the internet. Terrorist activity there, may be detected by analyzing web documents, downloaded by various groups of users. One of the main goals is to develop a model that will enable us to distinguish between a *normal* document that does not relate to terror, and an *abnormal* text which was either downloaded from an established terrorist website, or contains material that leaves no doubt regarding its hostile nature, thus reflecting on the person who received it.

Once equipped with a system that is capable of performing this distinction, we still have to determine whether a certain user that downloaded for example a single abnormal document should be already classified as suspect. This decision-making is a study by itself and should be based on accumulated experience by experts and experiments with real data. However, a necessary condition so that any policy related to pinpointing a suspect will be successful, is that the procedure of distinction between normal and abnormal documents, will be highly accurate.

The model represented in this work for detecting terror-related documents, is based on first replacing each document by a vector which consists of the most important words or expressions, called *key phrases*, that appear in the text. Each key phrase is assigned with *importance weight*, for example, the frequency of the term in the document. The replacement of a document with a vector of key phrases and importance weights is done by a special software called *extractor*. The efficiency of this tool in finding the right key phrases and assigning them the appropriate importance weights is a key feature in the performance of the detecting model.

In the next stage, the system accepts a large set of vectors, known all to be normal and cover all walks of life *except* terrorism. This is the *training set* of vectors which usually have different lengths and the model uses a fuzzy logic based clustering method to cluster them and create cluster-centers or *centroids*. The centroids are vectors that *represent* the associated clusters mainly for *similarity test* performing. An arbitrary incoming vector is compared with each of the centroids, using some predefined measure of similarity. If the vector is found similar to *any* of the centroids, it is considered normal. Otherwise, it is declared abnormal, i.e., this vector represents a terrorist document.

Clustering is defined as the unsupervised process of grouping a set of data objects into clusters of high inter-cluster similarity and low intra-cluster similarity [Baeza-Yates and Ribeiro-Neto (1999); Jain *et. al* (1999)]. Evaluating the quality of the clustering process is a highly subjective task, since it depends on both the similarity measure used by the method and the overall dispersion of the classified data [Baeza-Yates and Ribeiro-Neto (1999)]. Cluster analysis can be applied either as an exploratory tool (to discover previously unknown pattern in data), or as an input to a decision-making process. For the latter, it is reasonable to measure the clustering quality as the method's success to include an incoming object that *rightly* belongs to one of the clusters and to reject a vector which would be excluded by an expert. The main steps of a typical clustering process include object representation, definition of an object similarity measure appropriate to the data domain, grouping objects by a given clustering algorithm, and assessment of the output [Jain *et. al* (1999)]. In the Information Retrieval (IR) area, clustering documents is used in various applications such as determining the set of documents relevant to the user query [Salton (1989)], automatically generating taxonomy of document topics [Schenker *et. al* (2001)], Web activity monitoring [Last *et. al* (2003b)], etc.

Most popular clustering methods are limited by the assumption that every object is represented by a fixed-size vector of measurements. In this case a collection of n vectors is represented by an $n \times d$ data matrix where d is the total number of key phrases. The particular case of document clustering is usually based on the vector-space model [Han and Kamber (2001)], where each document is represented by a fixed-size vector of key phrase frequencies. Consequently, traditional clustering methods can be easily applied to matrix-based representations of document collections. The number of components in a document vector is equal to the total number of key phrases in the system, where a zero frequency is associated with each key phrase that does not appear in a particular document [Baeza-Yates and Ribeiro-Neto (1999)]. Since a document generally contains only a small subset of system key phrases, the associated data matrix is usually very sparse with up to 99% zero entries [Dhillon (2001)]. This generates a computational overload on the clustering algorithm unless zero elements are ignored throughout the computational process. However, although in general the clustering methods that assume fixed-size vectors are coded efficiently, they would usually not accept for example similarity between vectors of lengths 5 and 50. In other words the similarity measure of these algorithms is such that similar vectors are usually composed of more or less the same key phrases.

In this work, we propose a method for clustering web documents that are represented by vectors of variable size. The fuzzy-based approach for defining the similarity between documents, does not at all consider the vector's length. For each existing cluster we first define a centroid by *averaging* the vectors already classified in this cluster. The centroid is a vector that must include all the key phrases that belong to *any* of the vectors that are already in the cluster. However, the averaging function considers, for each key-phrase, only the number of documents containing that particular key phrase and not all the documents in the cluster. Then, for an incoming vector we apply an algorithm that computes its similarity to each centroid, treating each of its key phrases separately and assigning it a grade of membership within the cluster. In addition we also consider the current importance of the key phrase within the cluster by counting its current Inter Document Frequency (IDF) within the cluster's members. The vector will be classified at the closest cluster (i.e. the one with centroid to which the vector is most similar) provided that the distance of the vector to the associated centroid does not exceed a given threshold.

The definition of the clustering process, the cluster centroids, grade of membership of a key phrase in a new vector, the IDF of a key phrase in a cluster and the distance between a vector and an arbitrary centroid, are given in Section 6.2. An application in the area of monitoring Web documents is discussed in Section 6.3. The actual experiment executed by our system is given in Section 6.4, followed by summary in Section 6.5.

6.2   Creating the Centroids

Assume an ordered collection of documents. The usual process of unsupervised clustering is as follows. The first document starts the first cluster. Then, at any given moment, the similarity between an incoming document and all the currently existing centroids is computed. The document is assigned to the cluster with the most similar centroid, provided that this similarity measure exceeds a given tolerance. Otherwise, the new document starts a new cluster.

We now define the Inter Document Frequency (IDF) for a dynamic cluster, which measures the current *popularity* of a key phrase within the cluster. Assume a subset of n documents that belong to the same category. Each document is transformed into a vector that contains a maximum of m key phrases, also called *terms*. To each term we assign its number of occurrences in the cluster, i.e., its frequency in the cluster. At this point we do not take into account the importance weights of the terms, just the fact whether or not a given key phrase appeared in an arbitrary vector in the cluster. Thus, if a key phrase appeared 100 times or 5 times in a document, its IDF is equally affected.

However, we do not ignore the fact that a key phrase had multiple appearance in a document and we do count its frequency within the document as well as in the cluster. The result of compressing the n vectors together, is a matrix M of the form represented in the table above, where $\{V_i, 1 \le i \le n\}$ are the vectors that represent the document set $\{D_i, 1 \le i \le n\}$ and each f_{ij} is the number of occurrences of the term t_i in the document D_j.

Quite often f_{ij} serves as the only parameter for determining the importance weight of key phrase No. i in the j-th document V_j. This may not be the case whenever human expertise is considered as well as the term's frequency.

	V_1	V_2		V_n
Term$_1$	f_{11}	f_{12}		f_{1n}
Term$_2$				
...			f_{ij}	
Term$_m$	f_{m1}			f_{mn}

The cluster center, or centroid, could then be defined as the vector

$$c = \{a_1, a_2, \ldots, a_m\}$$

where

$$a_i = \frac{\sum\limits_{k=1}^{n} f_{ik}}{m_i} \tag{6.1}$$

where m_i is the number of vectors in the cluster which include the key phrase i (and not the total number of vectors in the cluster as done in traditional clustering). This average along with the maximum value of f_{ik}, are kept, in order to determine the *grade of membership* of this key phrase for new incoming vectors. Thus for each term in the cluster we store three quantities, namely, the *true* average of the term within the cluster, the maximum frequency of the term with regard to all the vectors and the IDB of this term within the cluster.

The reason for defining the average by Eq. 6.1 where the numerator is divided by m_i rather than by the total current number of vectors n in the cluster, can be demonstrated by the following example. Assume that in a given moment a certain key phrase t already appears in 20 vectors of the cluster with average frequency (in those 20 documents) of 10 but is missing in another 20 vectors (in the same cluster). If we obtain the average traditionally, it should be 5. Now, consider an incoming vector which is *likely* to belong to the cluster. If it contains t with frequency 10 this key phrase should be assigned grade of membership 1 since 10 is the most expected frequency of t in the cluster. However, if the average is defined as 5, than any method we apply for obtaining the grade of membership, must assign 1 for a new frequency of 5 and a number *less than* 1 to a frequency of 10.

As stated, the grade of membership of a key phrase t in an incoming vector with a frequency $f(t)$, which has the index j in the cluster, is determined by its average and maximum within the cluster, $f_{j,av}$ and $f_{j,max}$ respectively.

One possibility to define the membership $\chi(t)$ is by

$$\chi(t) = \begin{cases} (f(t)/f_{j,av})^p \ , \ f(t) < f_{j,av} \\ 1 - (f(t) - f_{j,av})(1 - q)/(f_{j,\max} - f_{j,av}) \ , \ f(t) \geq f_{j,av} \ , \ f_{j,\max} > f_{j,av} \\ (f_{j,av}/f(t))^p \ , \ f(t) \geq f_{j,av} \ , \ f_{j,\max} = f_{j,av} \end{cases}$$

$$(6.2)$$

where $p > 0$ and $0 < q < 1$ are tuning parameters and are application dependent.

This definition determines decreasing monotonic values from 1 to 0, when $f(t)$ varies from $f_{j,av}$ to zero. If $f_{j,\max} > f_{j,av}$, the membership decreases linearly from 1 to 0. It vanishes at $f(t) = f_{j,av} + (f_{j,\max} - f_{j,av})/(1 - q)$ which is a value greater than $f_{j,\max}$ which depends on the tuning parameter q.

Example 6.1   Consider a cluster C which already has 100 vectors distributed as follows: 10 vectors are equal to $\{(t_1,5),(t_2,4),(t_3,20),(t_4,10)\}$, 30 are equal to $\{(t_2,10),(t_3,30),(t_4,20),(t_5,8)\}$ and 60 are equal to $\{(t_1,10),(t_4,15),(t_5,12)\}$. Thus, the centroid will is defined as the vector

$$\{(t_1, 650/70), (t_2, 340/40), (t_3, 1100/40), (t_4, 1600/100), (t_5, 960/90)\}$$

which equals to $\{(t_1,9.3),(t_2,8.5),(t_3,27.5),(t_4,16),(t_5,10.7)\}$.

So far we ruled that the fact that a key phrase t does not appear in some vectors in the cluster does not decrease its average. This was done in order to obtain an appropriate definition for its grade of membership when appearing in an incoming vector. However, we must assign some importance to the fact that a key phrase, appears for example only in 50% of the cluster's members. In this case we could define the *importance* of t in the cluster as $1/2$ and consider this number in the final evaluation of the similarity between the incoming vector and the centroid. An extreme example that demonstrates the necessity for defining this 'importance' factor is the following. Let the current state of a cluster be that the key phrase t appeared (so far) only once, while there are already 1000 vectors in the cluster. Then, obviously, the fact that this same t appears in an incoming vector (even with the same frequency) should hardly have any effect on the similarity of this vector to the centroid. This measure of importance of a term in an existing cluster is known in the IR domain as IDF and is defined as follows:

Definition 6.1   The Inter Document Frequency (IDF) of a key phrase t in a cluster C is

$$\mu(t) = IDF(t) = \frac{number \ of \ documents \ in \ C \ with \ f(t) > 0}{total \ number \ of \ documents \ in \ C} \qquad (6.3)$$

Example 6.2 In the collection presented in Example 6.1 we have $IDF(t_1)=70/100=0.7$. However, the key phrases t_2, t_3 are less *popular*, since $\mu(t_2) = \mu(t_3) = 0.4$.

Thus, to determine the similarity between an incoming vector and an existing cluster, we assign to each key phrase in the vector a grade of membership $\chi(t)$, related to the distribution of t within the cluster (i.e. within the vectors in the cluster that include t) and a second grade of membership, $IDF(t)$, related to the *presence* of t within the cluster. If both numbers are 1 we obtain maximum similarity, based on this particular key phrase. If however, one of these memberships is very small, the particular key phrase should hardly affect the similarity between the vector and the centroid.

Definition 6.2 The *similarity* between an incoming vector v and a cluster C with centroid c is

$$sim(v,c) = \frac{[\sum\limits_{k=1}^{m(v)} \chi(t_k)\mu(t_k)]^r}{m(c)} \qquad (6.4)$$

where $m(c)$ is the number of key phrases that are in c and $r > 0$.

The quantity $1\text{-}sim(v,c)$ can be observed as the distance between the vector and the cluster center. The quantity r is a tuning parameter and as p and q that were defined previously in Eq. 6.2, is application dependent.

Example 6.3 Let the cluster C_1 contain the vectors

$$y_1 = \{(t_1, 8), (t_2, 24), (t_4, 6)$$
$$y_2 = \{(t_1, 8), (t_2, 30), (t_3, 10)$$
$$y_3 = \{(t_2, 12), (t_3, 22), (t_5, 10)$$

and let the cluster C_2 contain the vectors

$$u_1 = \{(t_1, 12), (t_2, 30), (t_3, 10)\}$$
$$u_2 = \{(t_1, 10), (t_2, 25), (t_4, 15)\}$$
$$u_3 = \{(t_2, 20), (t_3, 36), (t_4, 12)\}$$
$$u_4 = \{(t_3, 7), (t_4, 16), (t_5, 6)\}$$

Consider an incoming vector

$$x = \{(t_1, 7), (t_2, 19), (t_5, 8), (t_6, 10)\}$$

The centroids of C_1 and C_2 are

$$c_1 = \{(t_1, 8), (t_2, 22), (t_3, 16), (t_4, 6), (t_5, 10)\}$$

$$c_2 = \{(t_1, 11), (t_2, 25), (t_3, 17.7), (t_4, 14.3), (t_5, 6)\}$$

respectively. Assume the parameters $p = q = 1$, $r = 1$. The grades of membership of the terms in x with respect to C_1, calculated by Eq. 6.2 are $\chi(t_1) = 0.875$, $\chi(t_2) = 0.86$, $\chi(t_5) = 0.8$, $\chi(t_6) = 1$. The term t_6 does not appear in C_1 and we assigned it grade 1. This is irrelevant however, since $\mu(t_6) = 0$. The other IDF's are: $\mu(t_1) = 2/3$, $\mu(t_2) = 1$, $\mu(t_3) = 2/3$, $\mu(t_4) = 1/3$, $\mu(t_5) = 1/3$. Consequently

$$sim(x, c_1) = [0.875 \cdot (2/3) + 0.86 \cdot 1 + 0.8 \cdot (1/3) + 1 \cdot 0]/5 = 0.34$$

The grades of membership of the terms in x with respect to C_2, are $\chi(t_1) = 0.64$, $\chi(t_2) = 0.76$, $\chi(t_5) = 0.75$, $\chi(t_6) = 1$ and again, $\mu(t_6) = 0$. The other IDF's are: $\mu(t_1) = 1/2$, $\mu(t_2) = 3/4$, $\mu(t_3) = 3/4$, $\mu(t_4) = 3/4$, $\mu(t_5) = 1/4$. Consequently

$$sim(x, c_2) = [0.64 \cdot (1/2) + 0.76 \cdot (3/4) + 0.75 \cdot (1/4) + 1 \cdot 0]/5 = 0.22$$

Consequently, we assign x to C_1.

The similarity measure defined by Eq. 6.2 is certainly not unique. The main feature of *any suggested measure*, is, that it should, more or less, be in good correlation with the table in Fig. 6.1.

IF		THEN
IDF	**Grade of membership**	**Similarity**
low	low	very_low
low	medium	low
low	high	medium
medium	low	low
medium	medium	medium
medium	high	high
high	low	medium
high	medium	high
high	high	very_high

Fig. 6.1 Rules for similarity

Once an incoming vector is classified within an existing cluster, the centroid, the average and maximum values of each key phrase and all the IDF's, are updated.

6.3   Application

We tested our Fuzzy-based Clustering Method (FCM) on sizable sets of vectors that were created by an extractor from web documents. The preliminary results were very encouraging. Prior to describing the actual experiment we present the INPUT received by the code and the OUTPUT it provides after its tasks are executed.

6.3.1   *Clustering*

(1) **INPUT-1**: a set N of n normal vectors which represent web documents related to normal areas, i.e., documents that the people who download them or similar documents, are not likely to be involved in terrorist activity. The vectors are of various sizes and each vector consists of key phrases and their associated weights within the document.
(2) **INPUT-2**: a list of all the k key phrases within all the vectors in N.
(3) **INPUT-3**: a set T of n' vectors which represent terror-related documents.
(4) **INPUT-4**: a list of all k' key phrases within all the vectors in T.

The code performs fuzzy clustering on all the normal vectors of N and provides a set C of centroids, which represent all the normal vectors. The quality of the clustering can be determined by various tools from Pattern Recognition Theory, but the ultimate test is of course the system detection performance. The output prior to the detection stage is:

(1) **OUTPUT-1**: a set C of centroids, which are the clusters' centers. To Each centroid we attach a list of all the vectors in the cluster, a list of all the key phrases in the cluster, and each key phrase is associated with its average weight, maximum weight and its IDB value, all evaluated by dynamically scanning all the vectors in the cluster.
(2) **OUTPUT-2**: distribution of the clusters' sizes. One of the system's parameters is a number n-min which denotes the minimum number of vectors allowed in an arbitrary cluster. The detection performance certainly depends on n-min. A small n-min means fast detection, while a large value may cause some loss of information throughout the clustering process. Another important parameter is the distance threshold d. During the clustering phase, a vector will be assigned to the cluster with the closest centroid, provided that this minimal distance is smaller than d. Otherwise, the incoming vector starts a new cluster.

The code applied for clustering, uses the notation of distance rather than that of similarity. While the similarity measure varies from 0 to 1, the distance has the range from 0 to infinity. A zero distance corresponds similarity of 1.

To demonstrate the algorithm's performance we chose a Web mining application. Consider a large collection of web pages downloaded from the internet which cover many walks of life and can be defined as 'normal pages'. By using an available extractor, they are converted to vectors which are then clustered using the FCM method. Next we obtain a second set of vectors supplied by the extractor from web pages that are characterized by definite key phrases of anomaly. A good performance of the algorithm is achieved if the algorithm detects 'most' of the anomalous vectors by rejecting them from *all* the existing clusters.

6.3.2 *Detection*

Once the normal set of vectors is replaced by centroids, we may start the detection phase. Ideally, any normal incoming vector that does not belong to N should be classified at one of the clusters and therefore detected as normal. If this not the case for some normal vector x, the vector is referred to as *False Positive* (FP). On the other hand, we expect the system to detect a terror-related vector as such. If it is indeed detected as abnormal, i.e., if its minimum distance from all the centroids is *above* the given threshold d, we refer to the vector as *True Positive* (TP).

Throughout the detection phase, we present the system with n' normal vectors, none of which appeared already in the set N and with the n' terror-related vectors of T. It should be noted that the set T was supplied by an expert who downloaded its vectors from well-established terrorist websites.

We now let the minimum distance threshold d vary between d_1 and d_2. For each d we operate the system's detection routine on both normal and abnormal vectors of the two equal-size sets. We obtain two vectors of equal lengths of the corresponding FP and TP values. We plot TP vs. FP and this graph will demonstrate the quality of the system. The ideal state, FP = 0 and TP = n' for all d never occurs. A good system though will provide FP $\approx$ 0 and TP $\approx n'$ for a large range of d.

6.4 The Experiment

The set *large* set N for *training* the system included 16,400 normal vectors created from documents downloaded from a large variety of websites. The set T that represented terror-related documents included 100 vectors. The total number of key phrases was about 47,000 and about 50% of the key phrases in the abnormal vectors appeared in the normal vectors as well.

Before each computer run, we first randomly chose 100 normal vectors of N, for validation at the detection phase. The rest, 16,300 normal vectors were clustered and provided the centroids. After the clustering we operated the detection phase on the 100 normal and 100 abnormal vectors and obtained the numbers for FP and TP respectively for various choices of the minimum distance threshold d. We performed 100 runs and plotted the averaged results. It should be noted that the standard deviation of the TP – TF curves was small, i.e. the worst and best cases of the runs did not deviate much from the average curve.

The choice of parameters p $= 1$, q $= 1/2$ and r $= 0.3$ provided the results shown in Fig. 6.2.

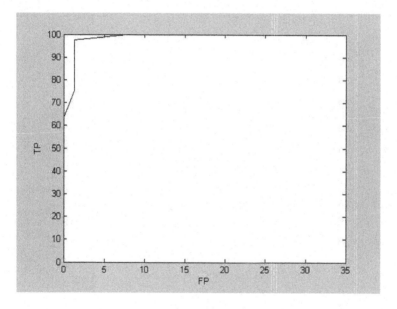

Fig. 6.2   FT vs. FP: averaging over 100 runs

6.5 Summary

In this work, we have introduced an algorithm for clustering documents which are represented by *variable size* vectors. The algorithm utilizes fuzzy logic to construct the cluster centers and provides a fuzzy-based similarity measure between documents. The system that was developed, based on this algorithm, for monitoring web documents and detecting terror-related documents, was applied to a large set of normal vectors. Following the creation of the normal centroids, we used the system's detection phase for detecting the vectors of two equal-size sets, normal and abnormal respectively. In spite of the fact that a large fraction of the key phrases in the terror-related documents appeared in the normal vectors as well, the code always provided reasonably good results. Future experiments will include increasing the pool of the terror-related documents, i.e., testing the system on a larger number of abnormal vectors, and incorporating a routine that will speed up the detection process.

Bibliography

Baeza-Yates, R. and Ribeiro-Neto, B. (1999). Modern Information Retrieval, ACM Press.

Dhillon, I.S. (2001). Co-clustering Documents and Words Using Bipartite Spectral Graph Partitioning, *Proc. KDD01*, San-Francisco, CA, USA, pp. 269–274.

George J. Klir and Bo Yuan (1995). Fuzzy Sets and Fuzzy Logic, Prentice Hall.

Grossman, D.a. and Frieder, O. (1998). Information Retrieval: Algorithms and Heuristics, Kluwer Academic Publishers.

Han, J. and Kamber, M. (2001). Data Mining: Concepts and Techniques, Morgan Kaufmann.

Jain, A. K., Murty, M. N. and Flynn, P. J. (1999). Data clustering: A Review, *J. ACM Computing Surveys*, **31(3)**, pp. 264–323.

Last, M., Shapira, B., Elovici, Y., Zaafrany, O. and Kandel, A. (2003). Content-Based Methodology for Anomaly Detection on the Web, *J. Advances in Web Intelligence, E. Menasalvas et al. (Editors), Springer-Verlag, Lecture Notes in Artificial Intelligence*, **2663**, pp. 113–123.

Salton, G. (1989). Automatic Text Processing: The Transformation, Analysis, and Retrieval of Information by Computer, Addison–Wesley, Reading.

Schenker, A., Last, M. and Kandel, A. (2001). A Term-Based Algorithm for Hierarchical Clustering of Web Documents, *Proc. IFSA / NAFIPS 2001 in Vancouver, Canada*, pp. 3076–3081.

Turney, P.D. (2000). Learning Algorithms for Keyphrase Extraction, *J. Information Retrieval*, **2(4)**, pp. 303–336.

Chapter 7

Analysis of Financial Intelligence and the Detection of Terror Financing

Yehuda Shaffer

Head of IMPA (Israel Money Laundering prohibition Authority)
The Israeli FIU at the Ministry of Justice[1], Israel
E-mail: shaffer@impa.justice.gov.il

7.1 Introduction

Terror groups are perhaps the most dangerous form of organized crime. Though not motivated by profit, terror groups must maintain a financial infrastructure to ensure their endurance. To do so they must use money laundering methods to disguise the source and purpose of their funds, especially when transferring funds internationally. Many of these transactions involve the use of cyberspace.

Attempting to detect terror financing activity, and specifically such activity over the internet requires an international legal and technological coordinated effort. Because most of the relevant information is in the private sector, any government monitoring of this information would require a detailed legal framework to ensure minimal infringement of civil rights such as privacy. Legal solutions will not suffice. A substantial technological effort is needed to enable detection of unusual or suspicious activity related to the financing of terror.

In this chapter we will describe the role of Financial Intelligence Units (FIU) in processing and analyzing financial data and intelligence, and detecting terror related transactions. The conclusions derived from this study can serve as a basis for public and scientific debate as to the future possi-

---

[1]The opinions expressed in this article are the author's and not necessarily those of the ministry.

bilities of monitoring the web for the detection of terror financing related activity.

7.2 Implementation of International Anti Money Laundering Standards in the Combat Against Terror Financing

7.2.1 The Impact of 9/11

In the past sixteen years, since the establishment of the Financial Action Task Force (FATF) by the G7 in 1989, focus has been put on the financial war against organized crime. Realizing the weaknesses of criminal law and both the failure to deter criminals and to reduce crime by the traditional puntative measures such as imprisonment, the FATF put the focus on the financial aspects of crime, and set a regime of international standards as found in the famous 40 recommendations to be implemented by each country. These standards include a series of measures meant to help law enforcement, identify the proceeds of crime, confiscate them, and bring to justice not only the criminals but those who helped launder their proceeds as well.

After the 9/11 attack an international consensus was reached as to the need to enhance global cooperation against terror financing.[2] Consequently the financial action task force FATF[3] decided to adopt the existing 40 AML recommendations as an effective tool against terror financing and in addition decided on nine special recommendations regarding terror financing. In 2003 the Egmont group of financial intelligence units amended its statement of purpose to include terror financing.[4] An impediment in combating terror has traditionally been the politicization of the issue, disabling the international community to reach agreement even on the definition of the concept of terror. Fortunately, with regard to terror financing, a common definition of terror has been agreed upon[5] in the International Convention for the Suppression of the Financing of Terrorism. This definition stigmatizes any violent terrorist activity against civilians with no exceptions as to "legitimate" possible motives (e.g. freedom fighters etc.) As a result the AML regime and specifically the information reported by the financial sector are now to be used in the combat against the financing of terror.

---

[2] UN Council Resolution 1373

[3] FATF Special recommendations on financing of terror see http://www.fatf-gafi.org

[4] The Egmont Group of Financial Intelligence Units STATEMENT OF PURPOSE of Guernsey, 23rd June 2004 http://www.egmontgroup.org/

[5] Article 2-International Convention for the Suppression of the Financing of Terrorism, 9 December 1999

7.2.2   Money Laundering and Terror Financing

There are several relevant differences between Money Laundering (ML) and Terror Financing (TF). In contrast to traditional organized crime the objectives of terror groups are usually not acquisitive. Many times they are funded by innocent legal donations and quite often there is a lack of clarity regarding the purpose of funds. Above all, terror groups, in contrast to criminals seek to operate outside the formal financial and banking systems.

Nevertheless there are several similarities between criminal and terror groups. Terror organizations use crime to raise funds and secure objectives. They share the characteristics of an ongoing criminal enterprise and their objectives are stigmatized as criminal. Furthermore, both involve international activity and use international financial tools. To conclude this point - a successful terror group, as any other criminal organization, is one that is able to build and maintain an effective financial infrastructure[6]. It is only logical that the regulations and institutions put in place to combat organized crime and money laundering will be utilized to fight terror and its financing.

7.3   Terror Financing Typologies

7.3.1   Characteristics of Terror (Not Only Terrorist) Financing

A common misunderstanding is questioning the ability of financial institutions or law enforcement agencies to track down the relatively small amounts of money needed by individual terrorists to execute the actual terror attack. As previously stated, terror organizations need large sums of money for maintaining organizational infrastructure. Such is the case for instance with the Middle East terror group of Hamas which maintains a network of "social welfare" (Da'wah) as a basis for its terror activity. Hamas utilizes this network to facilitate terror attacks, as well as to build grassroots support among the Palestinian population. Frequently, Hamas Da'wah operatives are the ones who ferry the suicide bomber and the explosives to the point of departure for the mission. Numerous Hamas members with terrorist track records are officials of Hamas charity committees[7].

Another point to consider is the cost of potential spectacular terror events. While the cost of the 9/11 attack has been estimated at $400,000,

---

[6]FATF — guidance for financial institutions in detecting Terrorist Financing) http://www.fatf-gafi.org

[7]Levitt Matthew, *Charitable Organizations and Terrorist Financing: A War on Terror Status-Check march 19, 2004*, The Washington institute for near east policy

one can expect that the cost of getting and operating Weapons of Mass Destruction (WMD) to be even higher[8]. To conclude this point, efforts should focus not on detecting the financial trail of the individual terrorist but on revealing the financial infrastructure of terror groups and their criminal enterprise.

7.3.2   Why and How Do Terror Groups Launder Money

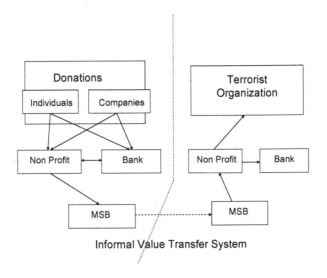

Fig. 7.1   Terror funding. A typical "money trail".

Terror organizations have been using all known techniques of money laundering. They do so for several reasons, but mainly in order to disguise the source and purpose of their funds and disengage themselves from their financiers. FATF has so far made nine special recommendations regarding the financing of terror, focusing on three relevant vulnerabilities of the international financial system regarding terror financing: Wire transfers, alternative remittance systems, and the abuse of non profit organizations. FATF called for Imposing anti-money laundering requirements on alternative remittance systems, strengthening customer identification measures in international and domestic wire transfers, and for taking measures to ensure that entities, in particular non-profit organizations, cannot be misused to finance terrorism.

---

[8]Allison, Graham. *Nuclear Terrorism: The Ultimate Preventable Catastrophe.* New York, NY: Henry Holt & Company 2004

Terror organizations use wire transfers to move funds intended for their activities. The financial support structure, revealed after the September 11th attacks in the United States, showed the essential role played by wire transfers in providing the hijackers with necessary financial means to plan for and eventually carry out their attacks[9]. Wire transfers do not involve actual movement of currency, but are a rapid and secure method for transferring value from one location to another.

The continuing development of world-wide networks such as SWIFT[10], has enhanced the reliability and efficiency of inter-bank payment systems, and when complemented by services such as telephone and internet banking, has added to the potential abuse by terrorist financiers and money launderers of such systems. The increased rapidity and volume of wire transfers, along with the lack of international standards as to recording key information on such transactions, in maintaining records and in transmitting necessary information with the transactions, serve as an obstacle to ensure traceability by investigative authorities of individual transactions. Terror groups have abused wire transfers by use of false identities, "straw men" or front companies in transactions to provide clean names and thus avoid detection. Another characteristic of their activity is to structure the flow of funds through several different financial institutions so that the wire transfers appear to come from different and seemingly unrelated sources.

In many cases terror groups transfer funds through non-bank financial institutions (Money Service Businesses - MSB) or alternative remittance services or by IVTS (Informal money or Value Transfer Systems) (see Figure 7.2) with the idea that by avoiding the mainstream financial institutions, their actions will remain undetected by financial monitoring systems or investigative authorities. In many cases transfers take place through non-bank financial institutions such as money remitters, bureaux de change or other similar types of businesses. These MSBs commonly perform wire transfer functions either directly with counterpart businesses in their own country or abroad or else through conventional financial institutions.

Non profit organizations have also been identified as vulnerable to possible abuse by terror financiers. It is therefore considered by FATF, a best practice for non-profit organizations that handle funds, to maintain registered bank accounts, keep their funds in them, and utilize formal or registered financial channels for transferring funds, especially overseas. Focus has been put on the need to verify adequately the activities of a non-profit organization. In several instances, programmes that were reported to the home office were not being implemented as represented. The funds were

---

[9]See interpretive note to the FATF special recommendations Supra note 3

[10]Society for Worldwide Interbank Financial Telecommunications. Network operation facilitating the exchange of payments and other financial transactions world-wide.

in fact being diverted to terrorist organizations. Non-profit organizations should be in a position to know and to verify that funds have been spent as advertised and planned (see Figure 7.1).

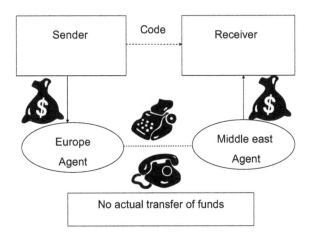

Fig. 7.2   Basic IVTS

7.4   Reporting Duties of Financial Institutions and the Role of Financial Intelligence Units (FIU) in Combating Terror Financing

7.4.1   *A Strategy for Fighting Terror Financing*

The abuse of the financial system by terror groups calls for a global strategy against this phenomenon. The overall goal of this strategy is to reveal the financial trail of funds used by terror organizations but it includes several separate goals to be achieved. First, the prevention of terror by freezing the assets of terror organizations planning terror operations. Another important goal is accumulating operational intelligence through the analysis of financial intelligence which would later assist in identifying terrorists and individuals involved in assisting them. A separate goal is the revealing of the sources of terror financing such as certain charities and shut them down. By involving the private sector in the combat against terror financing, terror groups should be alienated from the global economy, and others who might be inclined to support terror organizations will be deterred. Consequently, it is expected that terror groups may develop higher risk means of raising and moving money.

7.4.2 Information Received from the Private Sector ⟍

A key component of this strategy is the application of the anti money laundering standards and the reporting obligations imposed on the financial sector so as to include financing of terror as well. These standards include Suspicious Activity (or Transaction) Reporting (SAR or STR) and Currency Transaction Reporting (CTR) of any transaction exceeding a certain level (e.g. $10,000).

Financial institutions are expected to adopt Know Your Customer (KYC) procedures[11], if the financial institution has no reasonable explanation for an unusual transaction, this transaction should be considered suspicious and be reported to the FIU[12]. The Egmont group has categorized the possible reasons for suspicious reporting into six categories. Large-scale cash transactions, atypical or uneconomical fund transfers to or from a foreign jurisdiction, unusual business activities or transactions, large or rapid movements of funds, unrealistic wealth compared with client profiles, defensive stance to questioning.

These categories are especially relevant for banks but are applicable to other financial institutions as well. Focusing on alternative remittance services possible red flags that should alert the financial institution could be obtained either by study the customer, the transaction, or by other external circumstances.

Examples for red flags related to the customer are the use of false or multiple IDs, two or more customers using same or similar IDs or seem to be working together, comparison between the location of customer versus location of the financial institution, repetitive checks to same person from same or from other people on same or different accounts, companies with multiple addresses or bank accounts, companies with insufficient address (e.g.), unusual volume of activity, or transactions that are linked to suspicious persons or criminal elements (watch lists), or to organizations known to be linked to terror.

Examples for red flags related to the nature of the transaction are structuring (also known as "smurfing") of transactions into smaller transactions under the reporting requirement threshold, large or even sum transactions, untypical type of currency used, frequent transactions, transactions to or from abroad with missing details, transactions to or from NCCT or other non regulated territories, or the use of multiple bearer instruments.

Other external circumstances that should be examined are notations or

---

[11] Basel Committee on Banking Supervision Customer due diligence for banks October 2001 http://www.bis.org/publ/bcbs85.htm

[12] BSA Guidance for Bankers and Examiners http://www.occ.treas.gov/BSA/BSAGuidance.htm

initials on back of checks or money orders, improper endorsements, no endorsements, or repetitive endorsements, Small dollar checks versus fees paid (representing a high risk), checks dated months before or after date of deposit, checks suspected as forged or stolen (missing Signature), cases when client requests to exchange cash or check with a financial check, or with other check presented previously for discount, or use of checks of unique character (e.g. government, insurance).

7.4.3   *The Role of the FIU*

Reports of both STRs and CTRs are to be made to FIUs who are to be set up either as part of law enforcement agencies or as independent bodies (see Figure 7.3). As a result, investigating terror financing today depends much on the ability of FIUs to process and analyze large quantities of financial information, perform link analysis with other government available information and attempt to transform them into relevant knowledge linked to a criminal investigation. This can be achieved only with the convergence of high professional expertise of financial analysts and the sophisticated IT tools. Additional traditional roles of FIUs are to research terror financing typologies, educate the financial sector of possible red flags for STR reporting, and foster international cooperation.

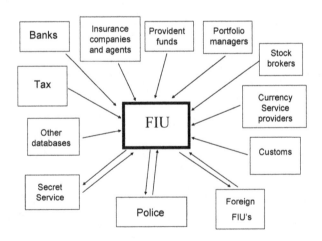

Fig. 7.3   Financial Information Flow

7.4.4   *IT Analysis Tools at FIUs*

Most FIUs have developed extensive IT tools to enable the efficient processing and analysis of suspicious transactions. One type of IT tools are alert generators, sold to financial institutions to assist them in detecting suspicious activity which should be reported to FIUs. These types of tools are also useful for the operation of the FIU itself. Alerts are generated through analysis of the FIU database focusing on the client, on predefined events, and on profile analysis. Customer analysis involves the study of customers, their behavior patterns, their connections to other customers and entities, and their potential risk factors based on information provided by the "Know Your Customer" requirements. Analysis of predefined events produce alerts when a pre-defined sequence of events is identified or when certain rules are met. A typical event would be structuring of cash or cash equivalents or circulation of funds between several accounts, including wire transfers in and out of the country. Profile analysis compares the recorded behavior of customers to other dynamic predefined profiles that are maintained by the system. Detection is based on deviation from the customer's historical behavior, deviation from peer group behavior, or similarity to a known suspicious behavior pattern.

Another type of tools are Enterprise Business Intelligence (EBI) tools which specialize in analysis of intelligence information, link analysis and data mining as well as basic information retrieval capabilities. All these features are combined and transformed into sophisticated visualization tools essential for analysts. Some typical features of such tools are the ability to access data, search through and extract information from a wide variety of data sources at once, visualize large quantity of financial transactions, identify and display relationships that exist between individuals and entities involved in terror activities, reveal connection between bank accounts and people, organizations, or other accounts, discover indirect relationships that show addresses, phone numbers, accounts or ID numbers with multiple users, and uncover different types of transactions used by terror groups using chronological and geographic data.

The Israeli FIU - IMPA (Israel Money Laundering Prohibition Authority) has for example been receiving approximately 400,000 CTRs per year (e.g. cash deposits and withdrawals exceeding 10,000 Euro) and approximately 3,500 STRs mostly from banks. This information has been processed and analyzed, compared with police and secret service information, and disseminated in approximately 150 cases per year to law enforcement for investigation of money laundering and terror financing[13].

---

[13]IT tools used currently at IMPA are http://www.actimize.com, http://www.svivot.com/

7.4.5 *Terror Financing Investigation*

A typical terror financing case investigated today includes financial intelligence, some of which was reported from the financial sector to the local FIU. Examples for such reports are the establishing of new shell companies and non-profit organizations and shifting of standing orders of monthly charity donations to their accounts, shortly after administrative measures were taken against the organizations to which donations were given before.

Analysis performed at the FIU must include careful examination of the financial documentation. For example SWIFT payment orders may include hints from the wording used by the donors for description of the charity purpose which may link the transaction to a terror group.

A major role of the FIU is performance of link analysis revealing mutual shareholders and controllers of companies and other entities linked to terror organization. Some cases involve the use of intermediates (e.g. public figures, attorneys) for deposits and withdrawals of cash to create a legitimate appearance. Another common characteristic is the use of charities, claiming that the money is for legitimate purposes, thus taking advantage of the lax supervision in many jurisdictions of regulatory bodies on Non profits.

Some cases revealed the use of structuring into small cash transactions (proving awareness by terrorists of the different reporting thresholds). Other cases involved the use of money orders and checks discounted by a money changer and then installed as a lump sum into the bank as part of their business thus not creating suspicion, and finally withdrawn with a bank check and deposited in an account of a different charity.

Other examples of financial activity FIUs seek to detect are transactions to or from uncooperative countries or by politically exposed persons, unusual high cash deposits, high level of activity of accounts that are generally hardly used, withdrawal of assets shortly after they were credited to the account, many payments from different persons to one account, repeated credits just under the limit, and fast flow of a high volume of money through an account.

7.5 Information Available - Possible Future Developments

As we have seen, information relevant for financial investigation of terror financing may be categorized into three types of information: Standard financial communication, Semi financial communication, and normal communication (e.g. Fax, Telephone, and Email) which supports the operations of informal value transfer systems (IVTS). Not all of this information is transferred via the internet, but a growing segment of it is. The financial information is of course coded and otherwise protected, whereas most of the other communication is not.

The standard financial information exchanged within the financial system include SWIFT and other payment and clearing systems such as CHIPS[14], TARGET[15] and CLS [16] as well as the more recent RTGS[17] mechanisms. These highly sophisticated networks serve mainly banks and large financial institutions.

Other existing Semi financial networks foster international communication between alternative remittance systems. Some of these are large legitimate operations of known international companies, and others are smaller private networks established as competition to the banking system.

Last but not least are the IVTS mechanisms. These use normal means of communications such as telephone fax and email, to balance payments made internationally. Actual cash is transferred by curriers only when necessary, but usually payments will balance each other.

Future developments depend much on the perception of the threat terror pose to world peace and security, and on the extent to which legislators and policy makers will allow security agencies to monitor activities in the private sector. Assuming the threat from terror will grow, several initiatives may be considered in this context. Legislators could either mandate reporting of more financial and communication activity to FIUs, or empower intelligence authorities to monitor critical communication and financial junctions and analyze the financial intelligence in the same way FIUs have been doing.

This intrusive potential invasion of privacy may be done using institutional or highly sophisticated computerized intermediates, serving as "black boxes" disseminating to the competent authorities only suspicious activity for further review. Suspicion could be determined either by a "hit" with Terror lists or when the information gathered regarding the transaction "fits" some known typology or pattern of money laundering or terror financing.

Another possible direction would be the planting of electronic "agents" within IT systems in the private financial sector or at different "junctions" of the financial activity, equipped with appropriate software tailored to

---

[14]Clearing Hourse In Tecbank Payment System.

[15]Trans-European Automated Real-time Gross settlement Express Transfer system. Interlink between the clearing system of the EU member countries with same day payment settlement.

[16]Continuous Linked Settlement: The global CLS payment system operated by some of the world's largest commercial banks, processes currency transactions in the major currencies according to the payment against payment principle.

[17]Real Time Gross Settlement system. Clearing system with irrevocable settlement of each individual payment without settlement of a counterclaim (gross system).

generate alerts to be reported to FIUs.

If so, tools must be developed for the monitoring of the flow of financial information, and the regular communication (fax telephone email) accompanying the financial transaction.

In addition several technical and legal issues must be dealt with. Standardization of the format of international banking transactions including the different banking clearing systems is essential for enabling processing and analysis of the valuable financial intelligence bestowed in them. Another issue is developing systems for character and sound recognition which can compare names and avoid spelling problems (Soundex) when comparing names to black lists of suspected terrorists or people involved in assisting terror groups.

Only time will tell if and to what extent policy makers shall enable monitoring of financial information transferred over the internet. Until then, IT tools should be further developed to enhance the ability of financial institutions and of FIUs to detect suspicious activity related both to Money laundering and Terror financing.

Chapter 8

Identification of Terrorist Web Sites with Cross-Lingual Classification Tools

Alex Markov and Mark Last

*Department of Information Systems Engineering,
Ben-Gurion University of the Negev, Beer-Sheva 84105, Israel
E-mail: markov@bgumail.bgu.ac.il, mlast@bgumail.bgu.ac.il*

8.1 Introduction

Terrorist sites are available on the net in different languages and can be viewed by almost everyone. Under such circumstances ability to detect terrorist sites automatically can be extremely useful. It can enable to reduce terrorist activity and propaganda on the web by finding and blocking those sites, detect users that request to download terrorist content online etc. In order to achieve this ability document classification[1] should be used.

Automated content-based document management tasks, generally known as *information retrieval*, have a long history and in early 90's became highly important in the information systems engineering due to the rapid growth in quantity of available digital documents. Classification is one of those tasks. Automated classification of previously unseen data items has been an active research area for many years. A lot of efficient and scalable classification techniques were developed in the areas of Machine Learning [Mitchell (1997)] and Data Mining [Han *et. al* (2001)]. Those techniques are used in wide range of applications and natural language, such as text and web, document categorization is one of them.

Document classification (aka *document categorization* or *topic spotting*) is the activity of labeling documents with a set of predefined thematic

---

[1]In this article Text and Web Document Classification is mentioned. Differences and similarities between those topics will be discussed in Sections 8.2 and 8.4.

categories. First document classification approaches were belonging to so called *knowledge engineering* domain. Categorization according to those techniques was based on rules generated by knowledge experts for each one of the categories separately. Such rule generation was very expensive and its prediction capability was low. Nowadays *machine learning* and *data mining* approaches are most commonly used for classification purposes. These techniques are using set of pre-classified documents to build classification model[2]. This model then is used to classify previously unseen documents. Classification accuracy of machine learning and data mining methods conventionally evaluated by dividing pre-classified documents into two, *training* and *testing sets* while training set used for model creation and testing set for validation. Each testing document treats as previously unseen, its label determined by model and compared to original.

Web sites classification became a very important sub-field of document categorization in last decade due to rapid growing of internet. Most web categorization methods come from conservative text classification techniques that use only inner text of documents for classification model creation. Such approach is not optimal for web documents. They totally ignore the fact that web documents contain markup elements (HTML tags), which are an additional source of information. Thus, HTML tags can be used for identification of hyperlinks, title, underlined or bold text etc. This kind of structural information may be critical for accurate internet pages classification.

Works referred to multi-lingual information retrieval mostly discuss problem of searching for documents relevant to user query, are commonly known as *query matching* [Aljlayl *et. al* (2001)], or machine translation techniques [Larson *et. al* (2002)]. Most existing works related to document classification have been validated with English language documents only. In fact it is difficult to estimate their performance for non-English document collections. Translation of documents to English with some machine translator is not recommended because of meaning deformation always caused by such.

In this work we studied the ability of a novel graph based classification technique [Markov *et. al* (2005)] to recognize automatically terror web sites in multiple languages. This chapter is organized as follows. In Section 8.2, we formally define document classification and its subcases. In Section 8.3, we describe the most important tasks to which web document classification has been applied. Traditional models of document representation are reviewed in Section 8.4. Sections 8.5 and 8.6 present the graph-based methodology for document representation and classification respectively. A

---

[2]Most popular data mining models will be briefly reviewed in Section 8.5.

case study with a collection of authentic Arabic web sites is described in Section 8.7 and some conclusions are given in Section 8.8.

8.2   Document Categorization and Classification

Document categorization may formally be defined [Sebastiani (1999)] as the task of assigning a Boolean value to each pair$\langle d_j, c_i \rangle \in D \times C$, where D is a domain of documents and $C = \{c_1, c_2, ..., c_{|c|}\}$ is a set of predefined categories. A value T (true) assigned to $\langle d_j, c_i \rangle$ indicates a decision to put document d_j under category c_i, and value F (false) indicates a reverse decision. In data mining two assumptions are usually taken by text categorization techniques: (1) the categories are just symbolic labels and no additional knowledge of their meaning is available, (2) no external knowledge, such as metadata, document type, publication date, publication source, is available – classification is based on document content only.

In some applications $|c|$ category labels may be assigned to each document. Cases when $|c| > 1$ are called *multi-labeled classification* whereas the case where exactly one category must be assigned to each document – *single label classification*. A special case for single label classification is a *binary classification*, where each document should be assigned to either category c or its complement $\bar{c}$. Terrorist web sites detection is a binary problem, because the goal is to classify document into *terrorist* category or its complement – *non-terrorist*. This categorization task has two problem features: (1) *unevenly populated categories* (much more documents belong to non-terror than to terror) and (2) *unevenly characterized categories* (e.g. what is about terror can be characterized much better than what is not).

In automated document classification *hard* categorization is typically used (T or F assigned to each$\langle d_j, c_i \rangle$), but some application may require to rank the categories in $C = \{c_1...c_{|c|}\}$ according to their estimated appropriateness to d_j. This approach is called *ranking categorization* and it is widely used in semi-automated classification systems.

8.3   Selected Applications of Web Document Classification

Web document categorization is relatively new research domain but its applications are already exist and widely used. In this section we will briefly review some of them. Much more applications can easily be found in the literature. Specific examples were chosen by us as more generic and important ones.

8.3.1 *Automatic Web News Extraction*

The number of web news portals has dramatically increased in last few years and so the quantity of publications and articles published on them. It is very difficult, costly in terms of time and occasionally even impossible for users to find news they are interested in. Web news are very frequently updateable so looking for news with query matching techniques is not efficient. Readers want to access news articles related to specific hierarchical subject like *politics (domestic politics, foreign politics ...), sport (tennis, socket ...)* and etcetera. Most electronic publications already separate their articles in set of categories, but classifications are not uniform.

Authors of [Maria *et. al* (2000)] try to solve this problem by creation of web-services framework that let users see published news on internet sites organized in a common category scheme. List of categories $C = \{c_1...c_{|c|}\}$ is defined first. Then $|c|$ classification models created using pre-classified manually training set of news sites. Each model i uses ranking categorization principle, which was explained in Section 8.2, to calculate appropriateness of document to category c_i. Afterwards news stories are automatically downloaded from number of portals simultaneously and classified.

News distribution systems became really popular nowadays. Articles are gathered from news web sites and displayed in browser window of PDA (Personal Digital Assistant - palm-top computer or mobile phone). Web document classification techniques typically used for choosing of relevant articles. WebClipping2 system described in [Carreira *et. al* (2004)] is good example of such technology. Interests may change over time, making it important to keep the profile up to date. The system monitors the users' reading behaviors, from which it infers their interest in particular articles and updates the profile accordingly. System retrieves articles belonging to 31 predefined categories. Determining of initial user profile executed as follows. Keywords relevant to each category extracted from big set of news stories when stopwords[3] are taken out. When users start using the system they must specify their interests in some or all of the several available subjects, with a value ranging from 0 to 100. A personal keyword database is built then as part of the user profile, by assigning to the words of each subject the value specified for it. This keyword database is necessary to the news classification process. Personal profile is then updated each time the user reads article by collecting the *hidden feedbacks* (reading time, number of read lines) and determining the interest of user in specific article. Naïve Bayes [McCallum *et. al* (1998)] algorithm is used in this work for classification purpose.

---

[3]Words without special meaning that cannot contribute to recognizing category automatically like *"and"*, *"not"*, *"the"* etc.

Another news gathering application can be found in [Reis *et. al* (2004)]. Extraction of relevant web news task is related to *information filtering* domain, that is very important research field in information retrieval and actively discussed in the literature [Amati *et. al* (1999)], [Tauritz *et. al* (2000)].

8.3.2 *Personalization and E-Commerce*

Web personalization is defined as any action that adapts the information or services provided by a Web site to the needs of a particular user or a set of users, taking advantage of the knowledge gained from the users' navigational behavior and individual interests, in combination with the content and the structure of the Web site. The objective of a Web personalization system is to "provide users with the information they want or need, without expecting from them to ask for it explicitly" [Mulvenna *et. al* (2000)]. The ability to do so is extremely important for e-commerce sites that are growing on daily basis.

Technically, web personalization is based mostly on web server log files learning. Most information about each user behavior on the web is stored in those files. The problem of these files is that they do not include content information about web pages user looking at. For instance, we have a rule: if user U visit page A he will visit page B also. Such rules are a core of personalization techniques and can easily be extracted from web logs files, but we can know nothing about content of pages A and B from those files. Here web classification is used for getting the content information of target pages and improving of personalization process. Good example of such a system is given in [Eirinaki *et. al* (2003)]. Document classification techniques are used by authors to expand the standard log files with site content information and improve personalization results.

Web personalization is very interesting and important for nowadays web systems research area that includes a lot of issues from deferent scientific and low fields. Most of those issues in context of web personalization are surveyed in [Eirinaki *et. al* (2003)].

8.3.3 *Organization of Web Document Collections*

Web site categorization became a major tool for organization of large document collections. The most popular examples of such collections are commercial, hierarchical organized, Web portals like Yahoo, MSN etc. When document is classified under one or couple predefined categories, it can easily be catalogued by one or more such portals. When web documents are catalogued in this way, rather than addressing a generic query to a general purpose web search engine, a user may find it much easier by first navigating down with categories hierarchy structure and then focus on searching only specific subcategory.

Solution for classification of web sites into hierarchical set of categories presented in [Dumais *et. al* (2000)]. It is based on simple assumption: if number of possible categories grows – classification accuracy goes down. So it is always better to separate classification problem into set of small problems with reduced number of possible classes by defining categories hierarchy. For instance if we have base category — *computers* and its sub-categories: *computer/hardware* and *computer/software* we will prepare three Boolean classification models in order to simplify this problem. First, second and third models will be trained to identify documents that talk about computers (in general), computer hardware and software respectively. This will give us opportunity to classify under hardware and software categories only documents that were truly classified as belonging to category of computers.

8.3.4 *Multi-Lingual Applications*

Multi-lingual document classification relates to case when documents, written in deferent languages must be classified under the same category labels simultaneously as opposed of cross-lingual classification systems that can work with different languages but not simultaneously. Those systems usually integrate machine translation technique with classification methods.

Multi-lingual *topic detection and tracking* (TDT) problem conversed in [Larkey *et. al* (2002)]. TDT is a research area interested in organizing a multi-lingual stream of news broadcasts as it arrives over time. Clustering[4] and classification techniques are used for topic detection. It is remarkable that initially each topic is represented with only a couple of documents in English. The streamed stories originate in different languages, but are also available in English translation. The translations have been performed automatically by machine translation algorithms, and are inferior to manual translations. At the beginning of the stream, native language comparisons cannot be performed because there are no native language topic models (other than English). However, later in the stream, once non-English documents have been seen, they can be used for tracking of native-language documents. This is done because of very important assumption in multi-lingual information retrieval called *native language hypothesis*. It says that if two documents organized in the same language, it would be best to compare them in that language.

---

[4]Clustering is the process of organizing objects into groups whose members are "similar" between them and are "dissimilar" to the objects belonging to other clusters

With the rapid growth of the Internet, the World Wide Web has become one of the most popular mediums for the distribution of multilingual information. Ability to distribute multilingual information has increased the need to automatically mediate across multiple languages, and in the case of the Web, finding foreign language pages. This is a *cross-lingual query matching* problem. Authors of [Aljlayl *et. al* (2001)] try to solve this problem for English and Arabic languages. The goal is to enable users to query in the Arabic language against an English document collection. To achieve this, query should be translated as accurate as possible. Couple of machine translation techniques are compared in the article in terms of retrieval quality. Solution for more languages are proposed in [Ahmed *et. al* (2002); Ripplinger (2000)].

8.4 Document Representation

Standard data mining classifiers get an attribute table as input for classification model creation. Each row of this table is a pre-classified data item and each column is an attribute of items, when particular cell is a value of attribute represented by column for a specific data item represented by row. Because of this fact documents in their original format can not be used as input for classifier and need to be mapped into such table. In order to perform those mapping, set of attributes common for all documents in training set should be defined. For text document it is a problem of choosing meaningful textual unit – term. In information retrieval techniques *vector space model* [Salton *et. al* (1975)] is typically used for document representation. Set of terms (features) $T(t_1, ..., t_{|t|})$ that occurred at least once in at least one document, serves as attributes and each document d_j is represented as vector $d_j(w_1, ..., w_{|t|})$ where w_i is a weight (significance) of term t_i in document d_j. Set T is usually called *vocabulary* or *dictionary*. Differences between various approaches are: (1) in the way of defining the term and (2) in the way of calculating the weight of term.

8.4.1 *Traditional Text Models*

In traditional information retrieval techniques single words are used as terms [McCallum *et. al* (1998); Weiss *et. al* (1999); Maria *et. al* (2000); Carreira *et. al* (2004)]. According to this approach, vocabulary is constructed from all words that take place in training set documents. Though this simple representation provides relatively good classification accuracy results, its limitations are obvious. This popular method of document representation does not capture important structural information, such as the order and proximity of term occurrence or the location of a term within the document. Experiments of join noun phrases and words in term set were done in [Tzeras *et. al* (1993)] and seem to be more effective in terms of classification accuracy. Since it is impractical and useless to insert all phrases into T set, only phrases that occurred more than three times in positive examples of the training set were used.

As to term weight calculation, *TF * IDF* (term frequency * inverse document frequency) measure [Salton *et. al* (1987)] is most frequently used and defined as

$$w_{ij} = TF \times IDF = TF_{ij} \times \log \frac{N}{n}$$

where:
w_{ij} = weight of Term t_j in Document d_i
TF_{ij} = frequency of Term t_j in Document d_i
N = number of Documents in collection
n = number of Documents where term t_j occurs at least once

Such calculation gives a highest weight to terms that occurs a lot in specific document but little in any other documents. The values of weight may be binary, indicating the presence or absence of the corresponding term, or non-negative real numbers, which indicate the importance of each term based on its frequency and other criteria.

8.4.2 *Web Document Models*

Most applications of web document classifiers still make use of standard text representation techniques that originally were designed for plain-text documents. There are couple of reasons why such approach is not optimal. First - text classification methods are based on assumption that no external knowledge, such as metadata, publication source etc is available. That is problematic for web documents since metadata is almost always available. Second and more important, web documents contain HTML tags which are not found in plain-text documents. These elements determine document's layout and can be a source of additional knowledge about the documents. Text documents representation methods are not aware of this important information. Representation that holds more information about the document will bring us to more accurate classification results.

In [Yang *et. al* (2002)] five different classification approaches were presented and compared. Typical vector space model was used for document representation but HTML tags were treated differently in each technique. First, *no hypertext* approach made use of web document text only for classification. No additional information was extracted from HTML tags. In *encyclopedia* approach, authors assume that all documents linked to the classified document relates to the same category and use its words as attributes for classification. The same assumption was taken in *co-referencing* regularity but words from original document receive higher weight than words from linked documents. Available information about already classified documents was used in *pre-classified* approach. For instance, if we know that document d belong to category c then it make sense that document d_1 linked with d can be classified under c too. In the last, *metadata* method only title and words under metadata tags are used for categorization. Experiments show that all methods that make use of HTML tags information have outperformed standard text representation technique. Disadvantage of those particular methods is that each of them is too narrow and their combination can provide even better results.

8.5 Graph Based Representations of Web Documents

In this section we introduce a novel, graph based methodology designed especially for web document representation [Schenker *et. al* (2005)]. The main benefit of the graph-based techniques is that they allow us to keep the inherent structural information of the original document. Before we describe the graph-based methodology, the definition of a graph should be given. A graph G is a 4-tuple: $G= (V, E, a, b)$, where V is a set of nodes (vertices), $E \subseteq V \times V$ is a set of edges connecting the nodes, $\alpha : V \rightarrow \sum v$ is a function labeling the nodes, and $\beta : V \times V \rightarrow \sum e$ is a function labeling the edges ($\sum v$ and $\sum e$ being the sets of labels that can appear on the nodes and edges, respectively). For brevity, we may refer to G as $G= (V, E)$ by omitting the labeling functions.

8.5.1 *Graph Structure*

When creating a graph model from the Web document, a series of pre-processing steps will be taken. *First* - all meaningless words (stop words such as "the", "of", and "and" in English) will be removed from text. Those words do not bring information about document's subject so they are not needed in order to classify or cluster documents. *Second* – stemming will be done to bring all words with identical stem into one form (e.g. "students" and "student"). Stemming, or normalization, is often used in information retrieval to reduce the size of term vectors by conflating those terms which are considered to be identical after the removal of their suffixes or prefixes. *Third* and optional is extraction of document's most frequent words. In order to reduce graph size and, as result of this, calculation complexity only N most frequent words can be taken for creation of graphs. The first two steps are language-specific, while the third step can be applied automatically to a "bag of words" in any language.

All graph representations proposed in [Schenker *et. al* (2005)] are based on the adjacency of terms in an HTML document. Under the *standard* method each unique term (keyword) appearing in the document becomes a node in the graph representing that document. Distinct terms (*stems, lemmas*, etc.) can be identified by a stemming algorithm and other language-specific normalization techniques. Each node is labeled with the term it represents. The node labels in a document graph are unique, since a single node is created for each keyword even if a term appears more than once in the text. Second, if word *a* immediately precedes word *b* somewhere in a "section" *s* of the document, then there is a directed edge from the node corresponding to term *a* to the node corresponding to term *b* with an edge label *s*. An edge is not created between two words if they are separated by certain punctuation marks (such as periods). Sections defined for the standard representation are: *title*, which contains the text related to the document's title and any provided keywords (meta-data); *link*, which is the "anchor text" that appears in hyper-links on the document; and *text*, which comprises any of the visible text in the document (this includes hyperlinked text, but not text in the document's title and keywords). graph representations are language-independent: they can be applied to a normalized text in any language. An example of a standard graph representation of a short English web document is shown in Fig. 8.1.

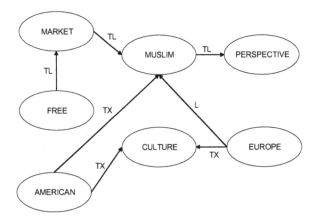

Fig. 8.1   Example of a Standard Graph Representation

The second type of graph representation is a "simple" representation. It is basically the same as the standard representation, except that we look at only the visible text on the page (no title or meta-data is examined) and we do not label the edges between nodes. Thus we ignore the information about the "section" of the HTML document where the two respective words appear together.

As shown in [Schenker *et. al* (2005)], the Standard and Simple graph representations can be modified in several ways. For instance the third type of representation is called the *n-distance* representation. Under this model, there is a user-provided parameter, n. Instead of considering only terms immediately following a given term in a web document, we look up to n terms ahead and connect the succeeding terms with an edge that is labeled with the distance between them (unless the words are separated by certain punctuation marks). For example, if the following text appears on a web page, "Children's sleepover in Cleveland", then we would have an edge from term *Children* to term *Sleepover* labeled with a 1, an edge from term *Children* to term *Cleveland* labeled 2, and so on.

It is possible also to use absolute or relative frequency for graph document representation. This is similar to the simple representation (adjacent words, no section related information) but each node and edge is labeled with an additional frequency measure. For nodes this indicates how many times the associated term appeared in the web document; for edges, this indicates the number of times the two connected terms appeared adjacent to each other in the specified order.

Using graphs we can add more useful information to web documents representation and expose a lot of new directions to research.

Available similarity measures between two graphs allow us to classify graphs with some distance-based *lazy algorithms*[5] like *k-NN* [Schenker *et. al* (2004)]. Computational complexity of such algorithms is typically very high. This is very problematic in terms of execution time and can not be used for online massive web document classification. On the other hand, we cannot induce even a simple classification model from graph structure using available data mining algorithms, which need an attribute table as input for the induction process. Consequently, graphs need to be converted into attribute table for classification model induction with some classifier. To achieve this, terms should be defined and extracted from presented document graph structure. In the next sub-section we will present two methods of term extraction.

---

[5]Algorithms that do not create model in order to classify data item [Mitchell (1997)]

8.5.2   *Term Extraction Methods*

Before term extraction methods will be explained, sub-graph and term should be defined. A graph $G_1 = (V_1, E_1, a_1, b_1)$ is a sub-graph of a graph $G_2 = (V_2, E_2, a_2, b_2)$, denoted $G_1 \subseteq G_2$, if $V_1 \subseteq V_2$, $E_1 \subseteq E_2 \cap (V_1 \times V_1)$, $\alpha_1(x) = \alpha_2(x) \; \forall x \in V_1$ and $\beta_1(x, y) = \beta_2(x, y) \; \forall (x, y) \in E_1$. Conversely, graph G_2 is also called a super-graph of G_1. In out representation methods, we define *terms* as sub-graphs selected by us to represent the document. Two optional term selection procedures are described below.

8.5.2.1   *Naïve Extraction*

All graphs representing the web documents should be divided into groups by class attribute value (for instance: terrorist, non terrorist). Then algorithm for frequent sub-graphs extraction will be activated on each group with a user-specified threshold value t_{min}. Every sub-graph more frequent then t_{min} will be chosen by algorithm to be a term (classification attribute) and stored in the vocabulary, for instance if $t_{min} = 25\%$ and frequency of sub-graph g in group of non terrorist documents is more then $1/4$, g will become an attribute of this particular group. All accepted groups of sub-graphs (classification attributes) will be combine to one set.

Naïve method is based on a simple postulate that attribute explains the category best if it is frequent in this category but in real life cases it is not necessarily true. For example if sub-graph g is frequent in more than one categories it can be chosen to be an attribute but can not help us to classify instances belonging to those categories. The "smart" extraction method has been developed by us to overcome this problem.

8.5.2.2   *Smart Extraction*

Like in the naïve representation, all graphs representing the web documents should be divided into groups by class attribute value. In order to extract sub-graphs relevant for classification of each group several measures should be defined.

SCF — Sub-graph Class Frequency:

$$SCF(g_k'(c_i)) = \frac{g_k' f(c_i)}{N(c_i)}$$

where:

$SCF(g_k'(c_i))$ — Frequency of sub-graph g_k' in category c_i.

$g_k' f(c_i)$ — Number of graphs that contains sub-graph g_k'.

$N(c_i)$ — Number of graphs in category c_i.

ISF — Inverse Sub-graph Frequency:

$$ISF\left(g'_k\left(c_i\right)\right) = \begin{cases} \log_2\left(\frac{\sum N(c_j)}{\sum g'_k f(c_j)}\right) & \text{if } \sum g'_k f(c_j) > 0 \\ \log_2\left(2 \times \sum N(c_j)\right) & \text{if } \sum g'_k f(c_j) = 0 \end{cases} \quad \{\forall c_j \in C; \; j \neq i\}$$

where:

$ISF\left(g'_k\left(c_i\right)\right)$ — Measure for inverse frequency of sub-graph g'_k in category c_i.

$N(c_j)$ — Number of graphs belonging to all categories except of c_i.

$g'_k f(c_j)$ — Amount of graphs that contains g'_k belonging to all categories except c_i.

And finally: *CR* — Classification Rate:

$$CR\left(g'_k\left(c_i\right)\right) = SCF\left(g'_k\left(c_i\right)\right) \times ISF\left(g'_k\left(c_i\right)\right)$$

where:

$CR\left(g'_k\left(c_i\right)\right)$ — Classification Rate of sub-graph g'_k in category c_i.

Implication of this measure is how good g'_k can explain category c_i. $CR\left(g'_k\left(c_i\right)\right)$ will reach maximum value when every graph in category c_i contains g'_k and graphs in other categories don't.

According to the *smart* method CR_{min} (minimum classification rate) will be defined and only sub-graphs with higher *CR* value than CR_{min} will be chosen as terms and entered into the vocabulary.

8.5.3 *Frequent Sub-Graph Extraction Problem*

The input of sub-graph discovery problem, in our case is a set of labeled, directed graphs and parameter t_{min} such that $0 < t_{min} < 1$. The goal of the frequent sub-graph discovery is to find all connected sub-graphs that occur in at least $(t_{min}*100)$ % of the input graphs. Additional property of our graphs is that labeled vertex is unique in each graph. This fact makes our problem mach easier then standard sub-graph discovery case [Yan *et. al* (2002); Kuramochi *et. al* (2004)] where such limitation does not exist. The most complex task in frequent sub-graph discovery problem is *sub-graph isomorphism identification*[6]. It is known as NP-complete problem where nodes in the graph are not uniquely labeled but in our case it has polynomial $O(n^2)$ complexity. We use *breadth first search* (BFS) approach and simplify the algorithm given in [Kuramochi *et. al* (2004)] for sub-graph detection.

---

[6]Means that graph is isomorphic to a part of another graph.

8.6   Cross-Lingual Web Document Classification with Graphs

8.6.1   *Representation and Classification Process*

Our process for cross-lingual classification models creation and classification of previously unseen document is shown in Figures 8.2 and 8.3 respectively. The first, model creation stage begins with a training set of pre-classified web documents $D = (d_1, \ldots, d_{|d|})$ and a set of categories as $C = (c_1, \ldots, c_{|c|})$, where each document $d_i \in D$; $1 \leq i \leq |d|$ belongs to one category $c_v \in C$; $1 \leq v \leq |c|$. Then parsing of HTML documents is done and all parts relevant for document representation are extracted. We used *standard* method for graph document representation as shown in Section 8.5.1, so relevant document parts are title and metadata, document text, and "anchored text" of hyperlinks. Next, document language is identified. This stage is needed because preprocessing stage is language-dependent. While preprocessing we remove from text all stopwords and perform stemming for remaining words. Obviously, stemming rules and stopwords list is defined separately for each language. In most languages, it is important to keep the original order of words in the document during graph creation [7]. Afterwards indexing is performed. During this stage we relate unique numeric index to each word and simply replace the word with its index. Original words and indexes for every language are saved in index files. Since we deal with multi-lingual documents and different formats (ASCII or Unicode) it is easier to convert words to uniform numeric format than handling the character set of each language. Next step is graph construction. Every document is converted into graph where we label the nodes with word indexes instead of words themselves and a set of labeled graphs $G = (g_1, \ldots, g_{|d|})$ is obtained.

Sub-graphs relevant for classification are extracted with either *smart* or *naïve* method presented in Section 8.5.2 and set of sub-graph terms $T(t_1, \ldots, t_{|t|})$ is obtained. Extracted sub-graphs are saved for previously unseen document classification. We represent then all document graphs as vectors of Boolean features corresponding to every term in T ("1" – a sub-graph from the set appears in a graph). Such vector collection can be transformed into one of conventional classification models. Examples of available classification models include decision trees [Weiss *et. al* (1999); Quinlan (1986); Quinlan (1993)], IFN - info-fuzzy networks [Maimon *et. al* (2000)], artificial neural networks, NBC — Naïve Bayes Classifier [McCallum *et. al* (1998)] and many others. Classification model for each language is the output of this stage.

Classification process begins with a set of previously unseen documents

---

[7]Examples of order-dependent languages include English, Hebrew and Arabic

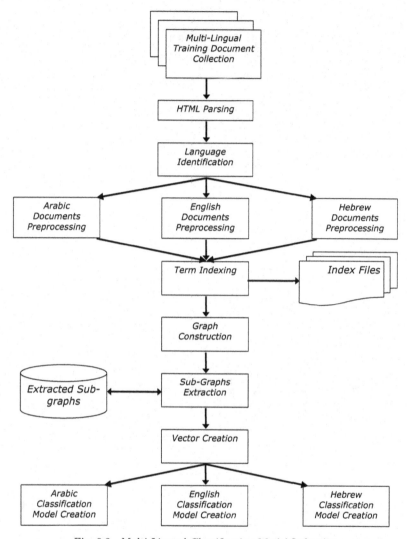

Fig. 8.2   Multi-Lingual Classification Model Induction

and first stages are similar to those of model creation process. A difference begins after construction of graphs. We use previously extracted sub-graphs as terms for vectors creation so we need to identify them in the set of document graphs. Then each document vector is classified with a classification model related to its language.

Index files can be used for converting sub-graphs back into readable structure by replacing indexes with words. It can help to understand which

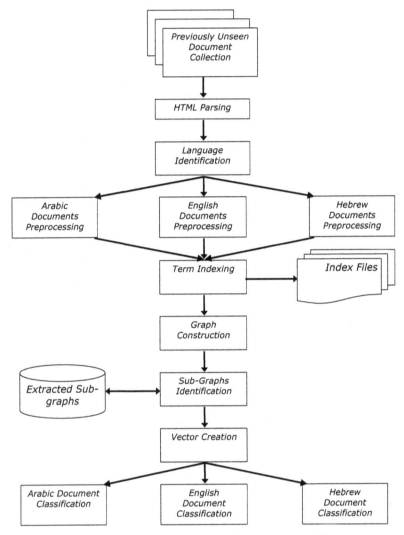

Fig. 8.3   Classification of Previously Unseen Multi-Lingual Documents

words or sentences were more relevant for classification than others.

8.6.2   *Web Document Representation Example*

In this section we will give a detailed example of our document representation process. Let us assume that the web document on Figure 4 must be represented as a vector for classification.

Iraq bomb: Four dead, 110 wounded

A car bomb has exploded outside a popular Baghdad restaurant, killing three Iraqis and wounding more than 110 others, police officials said. Earlier an aide to the office of Iraqi Prime Minister Ibrahim al-Jaafari and his driver were killed in a drive-by shooting.

FULL STORY

Fig. 8.4 Screenshot of a Real CNN News Page

Figures 8.5 and 8.6 show parts of HTML code behind this document. The complete HTML file is much longer and not demonstrated here because of space limitations and its irrelevance for the *standard* graph representation.

The goal of the parsing stage of our representation process is to extract the classification-relevant parts of the document which are, in our case, *title*, *text*, and *links*. The parsing output is shown in Figure 8.7.

After parsing, the document language is identified and it is sent to the language-specific preprocessing stage. Here stopwords should be removed and stemming is performed. All this is done while keeping the original order

```
<DIV class=cnnSectionT1
style="PADDING-RIGHT: 6px; PADDING-LEFT: 6px; PADDING-BOTTOM: 3px; PADDING-TOP:
3px">
<H2><A style="COLOR: #000"
href="http://edition.cnn.com/2005/WORLD/meast/05/23/iraq.main/index.html">Iraq
bomb: Four dead, 110 wounded</A></H2>
<P>A car bomb has exploded outside a popular Baghdad restaurant, killing
three Iraqis and wounding more than 110 others, police officials said.
Earlier an aide to the office of Iraqi Prime Minister Ibrahim al-Jaafari
and his driver were killed in a drive-by shooting.</P>
<P><A class=cnntllink
href="http://edition.cnn.com/2005/WORLD/meast/05/23/iraq.main/index.html">FULL
STORY</A></P>
```

Fig. 8.5   HTML source (document *text* and *links*)

```
<!DOCTYPE HTML PUBLIC "-//W3C//DTD HTML 4.0 Transitional//EN">
<!-- saved from url=(0023)http://edition.cnn.com/ -->
<HTML lang=en><HEAD><TITLE>CNN.com International</TITLE>
<META http-equiv=content-type content="text/html; charset=iso-8859-1">
<META http-equiv=refresh content=1800><LINK href="/" rel=Start>
```

Fig. 8.6   HTML source (document *title*)

```
<TITLE>
CNN.com International
</TITLE>
<Text>
A car bomb has exploded outside a popular Baghdad restaurant,killing
three Iraqis and wounding more than 110 others, police officials said.
Earlier an aide to the office of Iraqi Prime Minister Ibrahim al-Jaafari
and his driver were killed in a drive-by shooting.
</Text>
<Links>
Iraq bomb: Four dead, 110 wounded.
FULL STORY.
</Links>
```

Fig. 8.7   TheParsed Document

of the words in the web document. Figure 8.8 demonstrates the result of
this stage.

In the next, indexing stage each unique word is replaced with a numeric
index. Both words and their respective indexes are saved in the index file.
This is done to make automated graph building and sub-graph extraction
process easier, but graph nodes labeled with numbers will say absolutely
nothing to the human reader. We decided to skip this phase in our example
because of its trivial nature and poor contribution to understanding of the

```
<TITLE>
CNN International
</TITLE>
<Text>
car bomb explod Baghdad restaurant, kill Iraq wound, police official said.
aide office Iraq Prime Minister Ibrahim al-Jaafari driv kill driv shoot.
</Text>
<Links>
Iraq bomb: dead, wound.
FULL STORY.
</Links>
```

Fig. 8.8 Document after Preprocessing Stage

process.

The graph that was produced from our web document is presented in Figure 8.9. We set number of nodes to ten and used standard graph representation for this example as explained in Section 8.5.1.

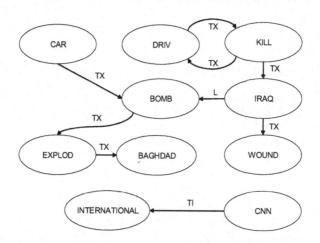

Fig. 8.9 Standard, 10 nodes graph representation of example document

Now let us assume that classification-relevant sub-graph terms collection contains 10 elements $T = (t_1 \ldots t_{10})$ and 3 of them are t_1, t_4 and t_5 (Figure 8.10) are sub-graphs of our document graph. If so, the vector of this document will be $d=(1,0,0,1,1,0,0,0,0,0)$.

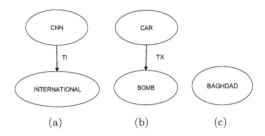

(a)   (b)   (c)

Fig. 8.10   Sub-graph terms (a) t_1, (b) t_4 and (c) t_5 (extracted from the graph in Figure 8.9)

8.7   Case Study: Identification of Terrorist Web Sites in Arabic

Our graph based representation technique has already been evaluated on three web documents collections in English [Markov *et. al* (2005)] with a lazy *k-NN* classification algorithm. In this work we present classification results obtained with ID3 decision-tree classifier [Quinlan (1986)] and documents in Arabic.

8.7.1   *About Document Collection*

In this case study we try to classify real-world web documents into two categories (Boolean classification approach): *terrorist* and *non-terrorist*. Our collection consists of 648 Arabic documents where 200 belong to terrorist web sites and 448 to non-terrorist categories. We took more non-terrorist sites because of Boolean classification properties that were presented in Section 8.2. The entire document collection contains 47,826 unique Arabic words.

Non terrorist documents were taken from four most popular Arabic news sites: http://www.aljazeera.net/News, http://arabic.cnn.com, http://news.bbc.co.uk/hi/arabic/news and http://www.un.org/arabic/news. We automatically downloaded about 200 documents from each domain and then manually chose 448 documents while checking that they are not belonging to terror category. We have also verified that at least 100 documents from each site are taken into group to ensure interspersion.

Terror content documents were downloaded from http://www.qudsway.com and http://www.nasrollah.org, which are associated with Palestinian Islamic Jihad and Hizballah respectively according to the SITE Institute web site (http://www.siteinstitute.org/). 100 sites were manually chosen from each domain and labeled as terror.

8.7.2   *Preprocessing of Documents in Arabic*

Text analysis for the Arabic language is a big challenge, as Arabic is based on unique rules grammar and structure, very different from the English language [Larkey *et. al* (2002)]. Orthographic variations are prevalent in Arabic; Characters may be combined in different ways. For example, sometimes in glyphs combining HAMZA or MADDA with ALIF the HAMZA or MADDA is excluded. In addition, broken plurals are common, so the plural form might be very different from the single form.

Another problem is that many Arabic words have ambiguous meaning due to the three or four-lateral root system. In Arabic, a word is usually derived from a root containing three to four letters that might be dropped in some derivations. Also, short vowels are omitted in written Arabic and synonyms are very common.

In Arabic, each word can assume a very large number of morphological forms, due to an array of complex and often irregular inflections. Furthermore, prepositions and pronouns are attached as an integral part of the word.

The first stage in text analysis is term extraction. We have defined a subset of Arabic characters in the Standard Unicode Table to be considered by the text analysis tool. The characters used are shown in Figure 8.11. The extracted terms are later stored in a data structure (array, hash table) which is called "term vocabulary". We tend to make the vocabulary as small as possible to improve run-time efficiency and data-mining algorithms accuracy. This is achieved by normalization and stop words elimination, which are standard dimensionality reduction operations in information retrieval.

Our normalization process for Arabic is based on the following rules:

- Normalize the initial Alif Hamza in the word to plain Alif,
- Normalize Waw with Hamza to plain Waw,
- Normalize the Alif Maksura to plain Ya,
- Normalize the feminine ending, the Ta-Marbuta, to Ha,
- Removal of Kashida (a calligraphic embellishment that has no associated meaning),
- Removal of vowel marks (the short vowels: Fatha, Damma and Kasra),
- Normalize original Arabic ("Hindi") numerals to their Western ("Arabic") counterparts,
- Remove Shaddah, which is a consonant doubler,

062	063	064
1	0	0
2	1	1
3	2	2
4	3	3
5	4	4
6	5	5
7	6	6
8	7	7
9	8	8
A	9	9
B	A	A
C		
D		
E		
F		

Fig. 8.11   Unicode values of used Arabic characters

- Removal of certain letters (such as: Waw, Kaf, Ba, and Fa) appearing before the Arabic article THE (Alif + Lam).

Next, each term was compared to a list of pre-defined stop words containing several hundred terms. If the term was not found in that list, it was added to the vocabulary of terms, provided that this term was not already in the vocabulary.

8.7.3   *Experiment and Evaluation of Results*

In order to evaluate our classification approach we used the ID3 decision-tree classifier. The goal was to estimate classification accuracy and understand how it is affected by user-defined parameters such as document graph size N, t_{min} in case of Naïve and CR_{min} in case of Smart approach. We used 30, 40, 50 and 100 nodes graphs in our experiment.

We used *ten-fold cross validation* method to estimate classification accuracy [Mitchell (1997)]. According to this method, the original training set is randomly divided into ten sections with approximately equal number of items. Then a classification algorithm is executed ten times while each time one different section is used as validation set and other nine sections as training set. Number of correctly classified document is reported as accuracy. Our experimental results for Naïve and Smart methods are presented in Figure 8.11 and Figure 8.12 respectively.

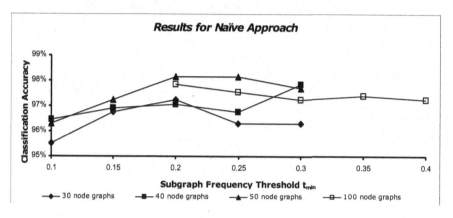

Fig. 8.12   Classification accuracy for Naïve Approach

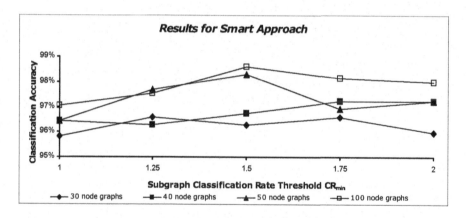

Fig. 8.13   Classification accuracy for Smart Approach

The best result for the Naïve technique was achieved with 50 nodes graph and 20% value of the minimum subgraph frequency threshold t_{min}. 89 subgraphs satisfying this condition were used as classification attributes. Only 12 documents out of 648 were classified incorrectly: 5 to terror and 7 to non terror category. For the Smart method, 100 nodes graph was found optimal bringing us almost 99% classification accuracy with the minimum classification rate CR_{min} value equal to 1.5. In this case, term set was made up of 218 subgraph terms. 5 documents were inaccurately recognized as belonging to terror category and 4 to non terror.

Figure 8.13 shows some real frequent subgraphs with Arabic labeled nodes that were chosen by *ID3* classifier as most relevant for terror web site recognition.

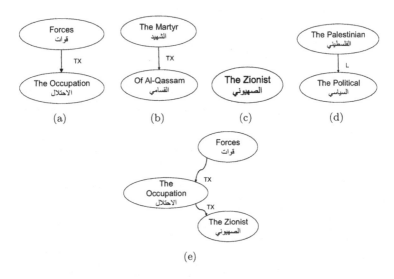

Fig. 8.14   Real life frequent sub-graphs

8.8   Conclusions

In this paper we explain the way document classification can help to identify automatically terrorist activity on the WWW. We also give brief overview of document classification with emphasis on Cross-Lingual Web Document classification. Our graph based classification technique was presented and its validation on a collection of real-world web documents in Arabic was performed. Our experimental results show that presented graph-based document representation methods can be used for high accuracy terrorist site detection on the Internet. Finding the optimal values of the Graph Size N, the Minimal Subgraph Frequency Threshold t_{min} and the Minimal Classification Rate Threshold CR_{min} using empirical and analytical ways is a subject for our future research.

8.9 Acknowledgment

We are grateful to Dror Magal, an expert in Arabic, for his valuable help with analysis of Arabic web sites and to Slava Kiselevich, a graduate research assistant, for his collaboration on execution of experiments presented in this chapter.

Bibliography

Ahmed, A., James, C., David, F. and William, O. (2002). UCLIR: a Multilingual Information Retrieval tool, *Proc. Multilingual Information Access and Natural Language Processing, Workshop of IBERAMIA 2002, in cooperation with ELSNET and RITOS-2*, November.

Aljlayl, M. and Frieder, O. (2001). Effective Arabic-English Cross-Language Information Retrieval via Machine-Readable Dictionaries and Machine Translation, *Proc. Tenth International Conference on Information and Knowledge Management*, October.

Amati, G. and Crestani, F. (1999). Probabilistic Learning for Selective Dissemination of Information, *J. Information Processing and Management: an International Journal archive*, **35(5)**, September, pp. 633–654.

Carreira, R., Crato, J. M., Gonçalves, D. and Jorge, J. A. (2004). Evaluating Adaptive User Profiles for News Classification, *Proc. 9th International Conference on Intelligent User Interface*, January.

Dumais, S., Chen, H. (2000). Hierarchical classification of Web content, *Proc. 23rd Annual International ACM SIGIR Conference on Research and Development in Information Retrieval*, July.

Eirinaki, M., Vazirgiannis, M. and Varlamis, I. (2003). Sewep: Using Site Semantics and a Taxonomy to Enhance the Web Personalization Process, *Proc. Ninth ACM SIGKDD International Conference on Knowledge Discovery and Data Mining*, August.

Han, J. and Kamber, M. (2001). Data Mining Concepts and Techniques, Morgan Kaufmann.

Kuramochi M. and Karypis, G. (2004). An Efficient Algorithm for Discovering Frequent Subgraphs, *J. IEEE Transactions on Knowledge and Data Engineering archive*, **16(9)**, September, pp. 1038–1051.

Larkey, L. S., Feng, F., Connell, M. and Lavrenko, V. (2004). Language-Specific Models in Multilingual Topic Tracking, *Proc. 27th Annual International Conference on Research and Development in Information Retrieval*, July.

Larkey, L.S., Ballesteros, L. and Connell, M.E. (2002). Improving Stemming for Arabic Information Retrieval: Light Stemming and Co-occurrence Analysis, *Proc.SIGIR 2002*.

Larson, R., Gey, F. and Chen, A. (2002). Harvesting Translingual Vocabulary Mappings for Multilingual Digital Libraries, *Proc. 2nd ACM/IEEE-CS joint conference on Digital libraries*, July.

M. Eirinaki, M. Vazirgiannis, "Web Mining for Web Personalization" *J. ACM Transactions on Internet Technology (TOIT) archive*, **3(1)**, February, pp. 1–27.

Maimon, O. and Last, M. (2000). Knowledge Discovery and Data Mining — The Info-Fuzzy Network (IFN) Methodology, Kluwer Academic Publishers, Massive Computing Series.

Maria, N. and Silva, M. J. (2000). Theme-based Retrieval of Web news, *Proc. 23rd Annual International ACM SIGIR Conference on Research and Development In Information Retrieval*, July.

Markov A. and Last, M. (2005). A Simple, Structure-Sensitive Approach for Web Document Classification, in P.S. Szczepaniak *et. al* (Eds.), Advances in Web Intelligence, *Proc. 3rd Atlantic Web Intelligence Conference (AWIC 2005)*, Springer-Verlag, LNAI 3528, pp. 293–298, Berlin Heidelberg.

McCallum, A. and Nigam, K. (1998). A Comparison of Event Models for Naive Bayes Text Classification, *Proc. AAAI-98 Workshop on Learning for Text Categorization*.

Mitchell, T. M. (1997). Machine Learning, McGraw-Hill.

Mulvenna, M., Anands, S. and Buchner, A. (2000). Personalization on the Net Using Web Mining, *J. Communications of the ACM*, **43(8)**, August, pp. 122–125.

Quinlan, J.R. (1986). Induction of Decision Trees, *J. Machine Learning*, **1**, pp. 81–106.

Quinlan, J.R. (1993). C4.5: Programs for Machine Learning, Morgan Kaufmann Publishers Inc.

Ramakrishna, K. and Tan, S. S. (Eds.) (2003). After Bali, the Threat of Terrorism in Southeast Asia, World Scientific.

Reis, D., Golgher, P., Leander, A. and Silva, A. (2004). Automatic Web News Extraction Using Tree Edit Distance, *Proc. 13th International Conference on World Wide Web*, New York, USA, pp. 502–511.

Ripplinger, B. (2000). The Use of NLP Techniques in CLIR, Revised Papers, *Workshop of Cross-Language Evaluation Forum on Cross-Language Information Retrieval and Evaluation*, September.

Salton, G. and Buckley, C. (1987). Term Weighting Approaches in Automatic Text Retrieval, Technical Report: TR87-881, Cornell University, November.

Salton, G., Wong, A. and Yang, C. (1975). A Vector Space Model for Automatic Indexing, *J. Communications of the ACM*, **18(11)**,pp. 613–620.

Schenker, A., Bunke, H., Last, M. and Kandel, A. (2004). Classification of Web Documents Using Graph Matching, *J. International Journal of Pattern Recognition and Artificial Intelligence*, Special Issue on Graph Matching in Computer Vision and Pattern Recognition, **18(3)**, pp. 475–496.

Schenker, A., Bunke, H., Last, M. and Kandel, A. (2005). Graph-Theoretic Techniques for Web Content Mining, Series in Machine Perception and Artificial Intelligence, **62**, World Scientific.

Sebastiani, F. (1999). Machine Learning in Automated Text Categorization, *J. ACM Computing Surveys (CSUR)*, **34(1)**, March, pp. 1–47.

Tauritz, D., Kok, J. and Sprinkhuizen-Kuyper, I. (2000). Adaptive Information Filtering Using Evolutionary Computation, *J. Information Sciences*, **122(2–4)**, pp. 121–140.

Tzeras, K. and Hartmann, S. (1993). Automatic Indexing Based on Bayesian Inference Networks, *Proc. 16th Annual International ACM SIGIR Conference on Research and Development in Information Retrieval*, July.

Weiss, S. M., Apte, C., Damerau, F. J., Johnson, D. E., Oles, F. J., Goetz, T. and Hampp, T. (1999). Maximizing Text-Mining Performance, *J. IEEE Intelligent Systems*, **14(4)**, July/August, pp. 63–69.

Yan, X. and Han, J. (2002). gSpan: Graph-Based Substructure Pattern Mining, *Proc. IEEE International Conference on Data Mining (ICDM'02)*, December.

Yang, Y., Slattery, S. and Ghani, R. (2002). A Study of Approaches to Hypertext Categorization, *J. of Intelligent Information Systems*, **18(2–3)**, March-May, pp. 219–241.

Appendix A

Useful Sources

Table A.1   This Book Web Site

Name	Fighting Terror in Cyberspace
URL	http://www.ise.bgu.ac.il/ftc/
Description	The official site of this book to be used for updating the list of useful links and other important announcements

Table A.2   Research Institutions

Name	ICT
URL	http://www.ict.org.il/
Description	International Policy Institute for Counter-Terrorism, Interdisciplinary Center, Herzliya, Israel
Name	Prism
URL	http://www.e-prism.org/pages/1/index.htm
Description	Project for the Research of Islamist Movements
Name	SITE
URL	http://www.siteinstitute.org/
Description	SITE Institute - The Search for International Terrorist Entities
Name	IDSS
URL	http://www.ntu.edu.sg/idss/
Description	Institute Of Defense and Strategic Studies - Nanyang Technological University, Singapore
Name	MEMRI
URL	http://www.memri.org/
Description	The Middle East Media Research Institute

Table A.3   Government Agencies

Name	DHS
URL	http://www.dhs.gov/
Description	US Department of Homeland Security official web site
Name	DARPA
URL	http://www.darpa.mil/
Description	DARPA - Defense Advanced Research Project Agency
Name	DIA
URL	http://www.dia.mil/
Description	US Defense Intelligence Agency (DIA)

Table A.4   Other Resources

Name	Financial Action Task Force (FATF)
URL	http://www.fatf-gafi.org
Description	The web site of the Financial Action Task Force (FATF), an inter-governmental body whose purpose is the development and promotion of policies, both at national and international levels, to combat money laundering and terrorist financing
Name	The Egmont group
URL	http://www.egmontgroup.org/
Description	The Egmont Group Financial Intelligence Units (FIUs)
Name	BSA Guidance for Bankers and Examiners
URL	http://www.occ.treas.gov/BSA/BSAGuidance.htm
Description	Links providing information and resources on BSA-related issues
Name	Infowar.com
URL	http://www.Infowar.com
Description	An information and computer security site founded by Winn Schwartau
Name	Arabic Information Retrieval
URL	http://www.glue.umd.edu/ dlrg/clir/arabic.html
Description	Arabic Information Retrieval and Computational Linguistics Resources
Name	MLIR
URL	http://www.ee.umd.edu/medlab/mlir/
Description	Cross-Language Information Retrieval Resources
Name	IAOC
URL	http://www.iaoc.org.il/
Description	Association of ISRAELI Old Crows, a nonprofit international professional association engaged in the science and practice of Electronic Warfare (EW), Information Operations (IO), and related disciplines

Appendix B

Terrorist Web Sites — Examples

- **Headline translation:** Pages from the Palestinian People Jihad
- **URL:** http://www.sabiroon.org
- **Organization:** Hamas
- **Language:** Arabic
- **Date:** May 10, 2005

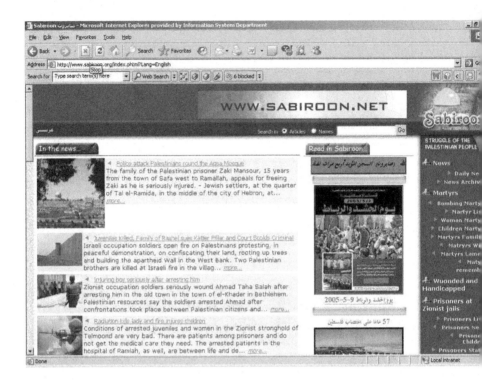

- **Headline translation:** Police Attacks Palestinians near al-Aqsa Mosque
- **URL:** http://www.sabiroon.org
- **Organization:** Hamas
- **Language:** English
- **Date:** May 10, 2005

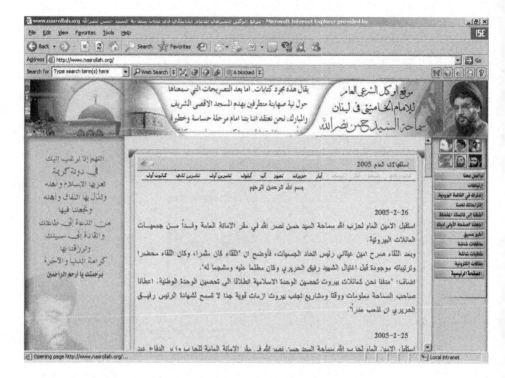

- **Headline translation:** Meeting of Nasrallah, the General Secretary of Hizballah in Lebanon, with Representatives of Families Living in Beirut
- **URL:** http://www.nasrollah.org
- **Organization:** Hizbollah (Lebanon)
- **Language:** Arabic
- **Date:** February 26, 2005

- **Headline translation:** The Organization Prepares for Commemorating the 57th Anniversary of the Disaster
- **URL:** http://www.qudsway.com
- **Organization:** Islamic Jihad
- **Language:** Arabic
- **Date:** May 10, 2005

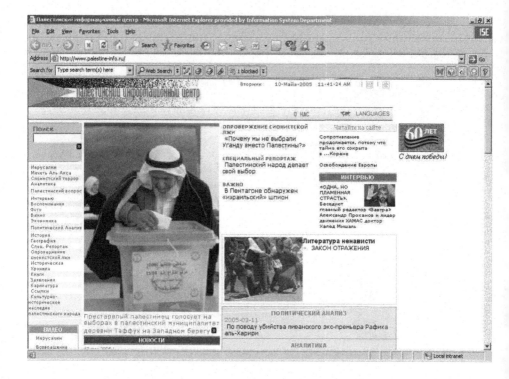

- **Headline translation:** Uncovering of a Zionist Lie
- **URL:** http://www.palestine-info.ru
- **Organization:** Hamas
- **Language:** Russian
- **Date:** May 10, 2005

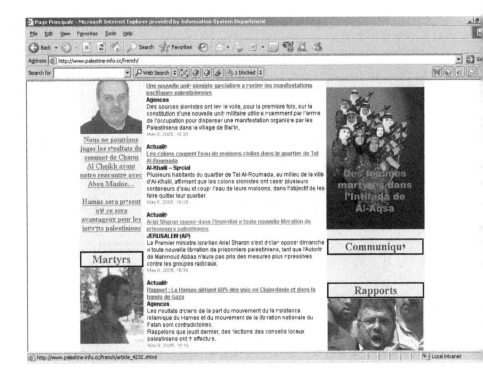

- **Headline translation:** A New Special Zionist Unit for Dealing with Palestinian Peaceful Manifestations
- **Organization:** Hamas
- **Language:** French
- **Date:** May 10, 2005

- **Headline translation:** The Zionist Occupation Attacks in Nablus
- **Organization:** Hamas
- **Language:** Arabic
- **Date:** May 10, 2005

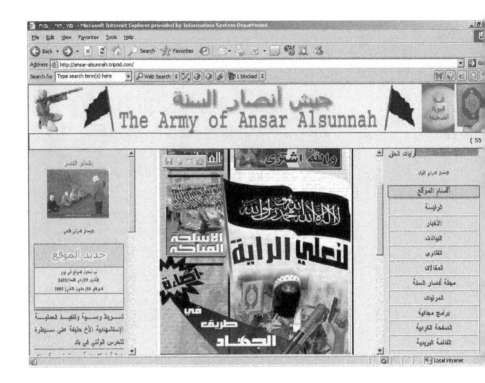

- **Headline translation:** In the Jihad Way
- **URL:** http://ansar-alsunnah.tripod.com
- **Organization:** The Sunnite Followers Army in Iraq
- **Language:** Arabic
- **Date:** May 10, 2005

Appendix C

About the Authors

Yuval Elovici

Dr. Yuval Elovici is a lecturer at the department of Information Systems Engineering, Ben-Gurion University. He holds Ph.D degree in Information Systems from the Tel-Aviv University, Israel. and B.Sc. and M.Sc. degrees in Computer and Electrical Engineering from the Ben-Gurion University of the Negev, Israel. His main areas of interest are computer security, internet security, information economics, and parallel and distributed systems.

Menahem Friedman

Dr. Menahem Friedman, born in Jerusalem in 1940, received his M.Sc. in Mathematics from the Hebrew University in Jerusalem in 1962 and his Ph.D. in Applied Mathematics from the Weizmann Institute of Sciences in Rehovot, Israel in 1967. During his postdoc, 1967 - 1969, he was an assistant professor at the University of Minnesota, Department of Mathematics and Computer Science. Since 1969 Dr. Friedman is a Senior Research Scientist at the Nuclear Research Center - Negev and during 1969–1992 held a part-time position as associate professor at Ben Gurion University of the Negev at the Departments of Mathematics and Electrical Engineering. Since Sepetember 2003 he is on sabbatical at Ben Gurion University, Department of Information Systems Engineering. Dr. Friedman's research activity is divided mainly between Numerical Analysis: designing algorithms for nonlinear systems related to control problems, 3-D Thomas-Fermi equation, excitable systems related to the heart — structure and operation and to heart diseases such as tachycardia, development of finite element software for solving mathematical models for various problems in Physics, Engineering and Medicine; and Artificial Intelligence: Fuzzy Logic, Fuzzy Differential and Integral Equations, Pattern Recognition, Software Testing and Web Mining. Dr. Friedman published two books, Fundamentals of Computer Numerical analysis and Introduction to Pattern Recognition co-authored with Prof. A. Kandel. He also contributed chapters to several books and published over 75 papers.

Abraham Kandel

Dr. Abraham Kandel received a B.Sc. from the Technion - Israel Institute of Technology and a M.S. from the University of California, both in Electrical Engineering, and a Ph.D. in Electrical Engineering and Computer Science from the University of New Mexico. Dr. Kandel, a Distinguished University Research Professor and the Endowed Eminent Scholar in Computer Science and Engineering at the University of South Florida is the Executive Director of the National Institute for Systems Test and Productivity. He was the Chairman of the Computer Science and Engineering Department at the University of South Florida (1991-2003) and the Founding Chairman of the Computer Science Department at Florida State University (1978-1991). He also was the Director of the Institute of Expert Systems and Robotics at FSU and the Director of the State University System Center for Artificial Intelligence at FSU. He is Editor of the Fuzzy Track-IEEE MICRO; Area Editor on Fuzzy Hardware for the International Journal "Fuzzy Sets and Systems", an Associate editor of the journals "IEEE Transactions on Systems, Man, and Cybernetics", "Control Engineering Practice", "International Journal of Pattern Recognition and Artificial Intelligence" (IJPRAI), and a member of the editorial boards of the international journals International Journal of Expert Systems: Research and Applications, The Journal of Fuzzy Mathematics; IEEE Transactions on Fuzzy Systems, Fuzzy Systems - Reports and Letters, Engineering Applications for Artificial Intelligence, The Journal of Grey Systems, Applied Computing Review Journal (ACR) - ACM, Journal of Neural Network World, Artificial Intelligence Tools, Fuzzy Economic Review, International

Journal of Chaotic Systems and Applications, International Journal of Image and Graphics, Pattern Recognition, Book Series on "Studies in Fuzzy Decision and Control," and BUSEFAL - Bulletin for Studies and Exchange of Fuzziness and its Applications.

Dr. Kandel has published over 500 research papers for numerous professional publications in Computer Science and Engineering. He is also the author, co-author, editor or co-editor of 46 text books and research monographs in the field. Dr. Kandel is a Fellow of the ACM, Fellow of the IEEE, Fellow of the New York Academy of Sciences, Fellow of AAAS, Fellow of IFSA, as well as a member of NAFIPS, IAPR, ASEE, and Sigma-Xi.

Dr. Kandel has been awarded the Fulbright Senior Research Fellow Award at Tel-Aviv University, 2003-2004, College of Engineering Outstanding Research Award, USF, 1993-94; Sigma-Xi Outstanding Faculty Researcher Award, 1995; The Theodore and Venette-Askounes Ashford Distinguished Scholar Award, USF, 1995; MOISIL International Foundation Gold Medal for Lifetime Achievements, 1996; Distinguished Researcher Award, USF, 1997; Professional Excellence Program Award, USF, 1997; Medalist of the Year, Florida Academy of Sciences, 1999; Honorary Scientific Advisor, Romanian Academy of Sciences, 2000, President's Award for Faculty Excellence, 2002. In 2005, Dr. Kandel was selected by the Fulbright Foundation as a Fulbright Senior Specialist in applied fuzzy logic, computational intelligence, data mining, and related fields.

Mark Last

Dr. Mark Last received his M.Sc. (1990) and Ph.D. (2000) degrees in Industrial Engineering from Tel Aviv University, Israel. He is currently a Senior Lecturer at the Department of Information Systems Engineering, Ben-Gurion University of the Negev, Israel. Prior to that, he was a Visiting Research Scholar at the National Institute for Systems Test and Productivity, University of South Florida, USA (Summer 2002, Summer 2003), Visiting Assistant Professor at the Department of Computer Science and Engineering, University of South Florida, USA (1999 - 2001), a Senior Consultant in Industrial Engineering and Computing (1994-1998), and the Head of Production Control Department at AVX Israel (1989-1994). Mark Last has published over 80 papers and chapters in journals, books, and conferences. He is a co-author of the book "Knowledge Discovery and Data Mining - The Info-Fuzzy Network (IFN) Methodology" (Kluwer 2000) and a co-editor of five edited volumes. His current research interests include data mining, software testing, and cyber security. Mark Last is an Associate Editor of IEEE Transactions on Systems, Man, and Cybernetics - Part C (since February 2004).

Alex Markov

Mr. Alex Markov received his B.Sc. degree in Information Systems Engineering from Ben-Gurion University of the Negev, Israel (2003) and he is currently an M.Sc. student of Information Systems Engineering at the same university. Hi is a co-author of "A Simple, Structure-Sensitive Approach for Web Document Classification" (Proceedings of AWIC 2005, Springer-Verlag, 2005). His research interests include data, web and text mining.

Moti Schneider

Prof. Moti Schneider Received his Ph.D. in 1986 from the Florida State University. He is a member of the school of computer science at Netanya Academic college. His area of expertise include: Artificial Intelligence, Expert Systems, Data Mining, Fuzzy Logic, Nueral Networks, Image Processing, Pattern Recognition. He published over 120 refereed papers and books.

Yehuda Shaffer

Mr. Yehuda Shaffer is the director and founder since January 2002 of IMPA — (Israel Money-laundering Prohibition Authority) the Israeli FIU (Financial Intelligence Unit) in the ministry of justice. IMPA is an administrative FIU which receives approx. 400, 000 CTR's (Currency transaction reports) (e.g. cash deposits and withdrawals exceeding 10,000 Euro (Approx.)) and 3,500 STRs (Suspicious (unusual) transaction reports) per year. This information is processed and analyzed, by competent analysts, compared with police and secret service information, studied on the basis of known typologies, and disseminated in approximately 150 cases per year to law enforcement for investigation of money laundering and terror financing.

Before that Mr. Shaffer served for 10 years as a Senior Deputy to the State Attorney in the High Court of Justice Department, in the state attorneys office in the ministry of Justice. Duties in this position included representing different government agencies in proceedings before the Supreme Court, and leading interagency teams in forming government policy on a wide range of issues, including law enforcement, national security, and various regulatory and economic issues in several government ministries. This position involved intensive cooperation with law enforcement agencies, especially the ISA (Israeli Security Agency) and the Israel Police. Mr. Shaffer participated in formulating and presenting Israel's position before United Nations treaty bodies, and participated (1998, 2001) in Israel's delegation before the Committee Against Torture (CAT) in Geneva.

Before that (1989-2001) Mr. Shaffer worked in a Law firm as litigating attorney in various corporate and civil matters. This position included negotiating various commercial, labor, and real estate contracts.

Mr. Shaffer received his L.L.B. and L.L.M. from the faculty of law at the Hebrew University in Jerusalem, and a masters in Public administration MPA - at the Kennedy school of government at Harvard.

Mr. Shaffer taught the course "Principals of Israeli Constitutional and Administrative Law", at the Public policy M.A. program in the Political Science department, Hebrew University of Jerusalem.

Mr. Shaffer served (1984-2005) in a paratrooper reserve unit of the Israel defense force (IDF) in various command positions, including 5 years as a regiment commander ranked lieutenant colonel, a position that involved the command of a paratrooper unit of 750 soldiers and officers. Before that (1980-1984) he served in the paratrooper brigade of the IDF as a soldier and officer, including participation in the Lebanon War.

Mr. Shaffer is the author of "The criminal offences in the prohibition of Money Laundering law — The international combat against money laundering in an Israeli perspective", Hamishpat Law Review, The College of Management, Academic Studies, Law School Publication, March 2005.

Bracha Shapira

Dr. Bracha Shapira is currently a lecturer (assistant professor) at the department of Information Systems Engineering in Ben-Gurion University of the Negev in Israel. She holds an M.Sc. in computer science from the Hebrew University in Jerusalem and a Ph.D. in Information Systems from Ben-Gurion University. Bracha's research interests include Information Retrieval (IR) and Information Filtering (IF), privacy and user modeling. Bracha leads theoretical and empirical studies that make significant contribution in the mentioned domains. The following is a partial list of some of her current research projects:

- Development of a formal model for information retrieval systems based on the Information Structure model, the formal model might be used for accurate evaluation of IR and IF systems and for their effective combination.
- Privacy preservation while browsing the Web, a prototype entitled PRAW- Private Web Browsing, was developed and evaluated and is based on dummy Web transactions to preserve user's privacy.
- Collaborative filtering using stereotypic inference. This research examines the type of stereotypic inference requires for accurate collaboration, and the effect of adaptation of the stereotypic groups on system's performance and users satisfaction.
- Collaborative filtering utilizing a market of evaluations. This research attempts to overcome the lack of evaluation provisions in collaborative systems. The economic model (the market) integrated in the collaborative system is aimed at generating intrinsic motivation for providing evaluations to improve the collaborative system performance.
  and others.

Bracha's numerous articles have been published in refereed Journals (such as JASSIST, DSS, IP&M, CACM). Her work was also presented at many professional conferences. Before turning to the academic world she gained professional experience while working as a system engineer and managing programming teams for telecommunication companies developing real-time applications.

Shaul Shay

Dr. Shaul Shay is the head of the Military History Department of the I.D.F. He is the lecture at Bar Ilan University and a senior research fellow of the International Policy Institute for Counter Terrorism (ICT) at the Interdisciplinary Center, Herzliya, Israel.

Dr. Shaul Shay served as a senior career officer in the military intelligence of the Israeli Defense forces and holds the rank of Colonel (Res).

He is a graduate of the Israeli National Defense College and completed both MA and Ph.D at Bar Ilan University in Political Science International Affairs.

Dr. Shay is the author of nine books and published many articles in Israel and abroad. Among his books are: "Terror at the Command of the Imam", "The Endless Jihad", "The Shahids, Islam and the suicide attacks", "The terror triangle of the Red Sea", "The Axis of evil", "Iran Hizballah and the Palestinian terror".

Abraham R. Wagner

Dr. Abraham R. Wagner, is President and a founder of System Research & Development Corp. (SRDC), a consulting firm specializing in national security and homeland security issues. He also serves as a Visiting Professor of International Relations at the University of Southern California, and as adjunct Professor in the School of International and Public Affairs at Columbia University teaching in the areas of intelligence, national security and technology. Dr. Wagner has held several positions within the U.S. Government since 1970, and has served with the National Security Council Staff, the Intelligence Community Staff, the Office of the Secretary of Defense, and the Defense Advanced Research Projects Agency (DARPA). Since 1980s he has also served on a number of Government advisory panels and groups, including the Defense Science Board (DSB); the CIA Scientific & Technical Advisory Panel (STAP), and others. In the late 1998-1999 he served as the co-chairman of an advisory panel for the Director of Central Intelligence looking into the evolution of the Global Information Infrastructure and its implications for the Intelligence Community. Following the 9/11 attacks, he served as the Chairman of a U.S. Defense Department (DARPA) panel looking at potential technology responses to terrorism. Since 2002 he has worked with several groups and the Department of Homeland Security developing technologies for counter-terrorism, and has assisted the International Policy Institute for Counter-Terrorism (ICT) in Herzilya, Israel with their annual terrorism conference and is currently the co-chairman of the Conference on Terrorism, Global Security and the Law sponsored by the Los Angeles Terrorism Early Warning Group. Among his numerous publications, Dr. Wagner has authored seven books, and co-authored (with Anthony Cordesman) a four-volume series Lessons of Modern War (Harper-Collins), as well a over 270 professional papers, research studies, and op-ed pieces. Dr. Wagner's has several book chapters currently in press on the subject of terrorism and related technologies.

Index

Accuracy, 83
activity monitoring, 93
al-Jazeera, 22
al-Manar, 22
Al-Qaeda, vii
alias accounts, 11
alias email accounts, vi
anomaly detection, vii
anonymity, vi, 32
ARPA, 2
ARPANET, v
artificial neural networks (ANNs), 45
association rules, 43
asynchronous communications, 6
automated testing, 47

behavior-based anomaly detection, 64
Bin-Laden, 35

classification, 55
classification accuracy, 118, 122, 123,
    138, 139
cluster analysis, vii, 44, 66, 67
clustering, 44
command and control, 7
communications, vi
communications intelligence
    (COMINT), 47
critical infrastructures, vi
cross-lingual, 122, 130, 140
Currency Transaction Reporting
    (CTR), 111

cyber intelligence, vii
cyber security, vii
cyber warfare, 7
cyber-attack, 26
Cyber-Jihad, 33
Cyber-Terrorism, 24

DARPA, 2
data mining, vii, 43
data visualization, 46
Dead Drops, 16
Decision tree, 45
Department of Defense, vii
descriptive data mining, 46
Dial-up services, 10
DIGITAL PEARL HARBOR, 25

email, vi
encrypted communications, 15
Encryption, 13
Enterprise Business Intelligence
    (EBI), 113

False Positive (FP), 100
False Positive Rate (FP), 83
Financial Action Task Force (FATF),
    106
financial intelligence, 116
Financial Intelligence Units (FIU),
    105
fuzzy clustering, 99
fuzzy logic, viii

fuzzy set theory, viii

grade of membership, 95
graph, 118, 125–130, 133–135, 138, 139

Hacking, 11
Hamas, 22
Hamburg Cell, 41
Hezbollah, 21
Holy Land Foundation for Relief and Development, 23
HTML, 67
hyper-text transfer protocol, 20

IEDs, 19
IMPA (Israel Money Laundering Prohibition Authority), 113
improvised explosive devices, 19
Info-Fuzzy Network (IFN), 45
informal value transfer systems (IVTS), 114
Information Agents, 49
Information Retrieval (IR), 93
information signature, 46
Information Terrorism, 31
Input-Output Analysis, 56
intelligence, vi
Inter Document Frequency (IDF), 96
Internet cafes, v
IP address, 65
Islam, 29
Islamic Association for Palestine, 22
IVTS (Informal money or Value Transfer Systems), 109
Izz al-Din al-Kassam Brigades, 22

jihad, vi

K-Means clustering, 82
K-Nearest Neighbor (k-NN), 45
key phrase, 95
Know Your Customer (KYC), 111
knowledge discovery in databases (KDD), 43

Lebanon, 22
Link analysis, 46
logic bombs, 56
Logistics, 18

M-IFN, 57
meta-search agents, 46
Mohammed Atta, 42
money laundering, viii
Money Laundering (ML), 107
Moores Law, 5
multi-output data mining algorithm, 57
Muslim Students Association, 22

Naive Bayes Classifier (NBC), 45
National Security Agency, 25
netwar, 33

Online-HTML Tracer (OHT), 79
ontology, 51
Osama bin Laden, 21

Packet Switching, 5
Page loss rate (PLR), 83
Palestinian Islamic Jihad (PIJ), 22
Pattern Recognition, 99
Predictive, 44
predictive modeling, 44
privacy, 18
propaganda, vi
psychological operations (PSYOP), 34
psychological warfare, vii

real-time data mining, 47
Regression, 45
regression testing, 56
ROC curves, 84

smurfing, 111
social welfare (*Da'wah*), 107
Soundex, 116
spoof, vi
Steganography, 16
sub-graph extraction, 129, 134

Summarization, 60
Suspicious Activity (or Transaction)
   Reporting (SAR or STR), 111
SWIFT, 114

terror financing, viii
Terror Financing (TF), 107
Terrorist Detection System (TDS), 76
Terrorist Propaganda, 21
TF * IDF, 124
The Palestinian Authority (PA), 22
trend discovery, 47
True Positive (TP), 100
True Positive Rate (TP), 83

URLs, 84

vector space model, 123, 124
visual data analysis, 46

web documents, vii
Web mining, 100
web sites, vii
web-crawling, 46
Wire transfers, 108
Wireless Internet, 11

Printed in the United States
By Bookmasters